YOUR KNOWLEDGE HAS VALUE

- We will publish your bachelor's and master's thesis, essays and papers

- Your own eBook and book - sold worldwide in all relevant shops

- Earn money with each sale

Upload your text at www.GRIN.com and publish for free

Asheesh Shanker

The programming language "Perl" for Biologists

Solutions for Beginners

GRIN Publishing

Bibliographic information published by the German National Library:

The German National Library lists this publication in the National Bibliography; detailed bibliographic data are available on the Internet at http://dnb.dnb.de .

This book is copyright material and must not be copied, reproduced, transferred, distributed, leased, licensed or publicly performed or used in any way except as specifically permitted in writing by the publishers, as allowed under the terms and conditions under which it was purchased or as strictly permitted by applicable copyright law. Any unauthorized distribution or use of this text may be a direct infringement of the author s and publisher s rights and those responsible may be liable in law accordingly.

Imprint:

Copyright © 2015 GRIN Verlag GmbH
Print and binding: Books on Demand GmbH, Norderstedt Germany
ISBN: 978-3-656-90770-1

This book at GRIN:

http://www.grin.com/en/e-book/293272/the-programming-language-perl-for-bio-logists

GRIN - Your knowledge has value

Since its foundation in 1998, GRIN has specialized in publishing academic texts by students, college teachers and other academics as e-book and printed book. The website www.grin.com is an ideal platform for presenting term papers, final papers, scientific essays, dissertations and specialist books.

Visit us on the internet:

http://www.grin.com/

http://www.facebook.com/grincom

http://www.twitter.com/grin_com

The Programming Language "Perl" for Biologists Solutions for Beginners

Asheesh Shanker

Asheesh Shanker
M.Sc., Ph.D. (Bioinformatics)
Associate Professor
Dept. of Biosciences and Biotechnology
Banasthali University - 304022
Rajasthan, India

To my daughter Akshita (Pearl)

About the book

This book is designed to be useful in theory and practical classes of UG and PG bioinformatics students. Moreover, it will be beneficial to other persons who wish to learn Perl programming language. To explain the Perl jargon, program based approach is used throughout the book. Important points are provided at the end of each chapter along with questions to test the skills. Solutions of find errors are provided at the end of the book. All the programs are tested on Windows 7 with Perl v5.18.1.

The book is divided into thirteen chapters which gradually take a reader from basic to advanced Perl. Although the book has been drafted with utmost care, it is quite possible that some errors/misprints might have crept in the book. I request the readers for their valuable suggestions and comments for further improvement of the book.

Acknowledgements

To my teachers, students, family, friends, and The Architect of Universe.

Preface

The interdisciplinary field of bioinformatics establishes itself as an indispensible branch of science. It is impossible to conduct the high throughput biological studies without the involvement of bioinformatics. Even it is difficult to imagine large scale biological projects which do not use any bioinformatics tool. To fulfill this requirement bioinformaticians have developed several tools that can help in the study of genomics, proteomics, metabolomics and other areas of biological sciences. Apart from this a large number of biological databases have also been developed which are sometimes a byproduct of high throughput research. Programming languages play a very important role in these developments.

Practical Extraction and Report Language (PERL) proved to be one of the most useful programming languages in such projects including the human genome sequencing project. The pattern matching and parsing capabilities of Perl suits the tasks required in biological science research which makes it a choice of bio-programmers. Researchers and academicians are extensively using Perl in devising programming solutions for problems related to biological data. Ever since Perl is one of the most important programming languages for a bioinformatician, therefore, throughout the country Perl is included as a core component in the syllabi of UG and PG courses in bioinformatics. During my teaching experience I found that students of diverse backgrounds opt for bioinformatics courses. Among them the students with biological background face lots of difficulty in learning programming languages. This prompted me to undertake this exciting, challenging project and put my several years of teaching and research experience in it. Perl for Biologists: Solutions for Beginners has been written keeping in view the requirements of Perl readers and incorporating the syllabi of the UG and PG bioinformatics courses of various Indian universities. I tried to express Perl in an easy, understandable language through lots of programming solutions which can be comfortably grasped by the learners. The layout of the book ensures that the readers can easily understand the given concepts without having prior knowledge of programming languages. I hope this book comes out as a useful publication. Enjoy Programming!!!

Contents

List of Perl Programs

Advice Before You Start

- Have patience.
- Carefully read the warnings and error messages.

Chapter 1

Introduction (Quick start)

- PERL is an acronym of Practical Extraction and Report Language developed by Larry Wall in 1987.

- Perl is freely available as a part of various operating system distributions (Linux, Mac etc.) and can be easily installed on Windows OS.

- To check the version of Perl installed on your system type perl –v followed by enter on command prompt (Start → Accessories → Command Prompt) and it will show you the installed version, if any.

 C:\Users\BI> perl -v

Output:
This is Perl 5, version 18, subversion 1 (v5.18.1) built for MSWin32-x86-multi-thread-64int

Copyright 1987-2013, Larry Wall

Perl may be copied only under the terms of either the Artistic License or the GNU General Public License, which may be found in the Perl 5 source kit.

Complete documentation for Perl, including FAQ lists, should be found on this system using "man Perl" or "Perldoc Perl". If you have access to the Internet, point your browser at http://www.Perl.org/, the Perl Home Page.

- It is a case-sensitive, interpreter based, procedural programming language but can also be used to write programs in object oriented programming paradigm.

- Perl works with the motto that "There's more than one way to do it."

- To start with Perl open a text editor (Notepad in Windows and vim in Linux) and type following lines

  print "Hello there";

save the file with filename "first_ program.pl". To execute this Perl program type perl first_ program.pl on command prompt

---

Program 1.1
Test program

#My first Perl program ◄——— Comment
print "Hello there";   ◄——— Perl statement

Execution: C:\Users\BI> perl first_ program.pl

Output:
Hello there

- It is good to write comments in your program. A # sign is used to write comment in Perl and interpreter skips the text written after this sign.

- In this program the print function has been used to display the string (Hello there) on standard output (monitor).

- Almost all statements in Perl end with a semicolon (;).

- Windows users take care if Perl is not in the system path then save the program in Perl/bin folder where the interpreter will be present. Perl folder will be present in the directory where Perl has been installed.

- It is a good practice to save Perl programs with .pl extension and the program name must be related to the problem for which program is written. For example, substring.pl is a suitable name for a program that can be used to retrieve a substring from a string.

Points to remember

- Usually beginners do mistake by not remembering the location of program where it is saved. When program has been executed from any other location where it is not stored, an error message similar to "Can't open Perl script "ProgramName.pl": No such file or directory" appears on the command prompt.
- Always remember the location of the stored program. After opening the command prompt navigate to the same location where the program is stored then execute it.
- Type the program name correctly. Incorrect name leads to error message.
- Check whether Perl is present in system path. If not, ask system administrator to include it in the system path, otherwise save the program in Perl/bin folder and execute.

Test Yourself

1. Write a program to print your name.
2. Write a program to print your class.
3. Write a program to print the name of your institute.
4. Write a program to print your age.

Find errors

Program E1.1

#My first Perl program
print "Hello there;

Output:
Error message

Program E1.2

#My first Perl program
Print "Hello there";

Output:
Error message

Chapter 2

Variables and Data Formatting

- Variables are used to store data (Characters, alphanumeric characters or numbers) therefore act as data containers.
- A variable name refers to the memory location where data is stored in the computer's memory.
- There are three variables commonly used in Perl. These are Scalar, Array and Associative array or hash.
- Perl recognizes the type of variable using the symbol prefixing the variable name.
    - Scalar variables are represented by prefixing $ sign with variable name.
    - Array is represented using @ sign.
    - Associative array or hash is represented by % sign.
- Assignment operator (equal to sign; =) is used to assign value to a variable. It assigns a value on its right to a variable on its left.
- Variable names are case sensitive. For example, $string and $STRING are different scalar variables.

Program 2.1

```
# Program to check case sensitivity of variables name
use strict;
use warnings;

#Variable names are case sensitive
my $string = 'Biology';
my $STRING = 'Bioinformatics';
```

```
print $string," and ", $STRING;
```

Output:
Biology and Bioinformatics

Explanation: The lines beginning with # are comments in this program. Strict and warnings are Perl pragma to restrict unsafe constructs and control optional warnings, respectively. A pragma is a module which influences some aspect of the run time behavior of Perl. Make a habit to use these two pragmas in your programs to write a well-organized code. Use of my keyword with a variable name (my $string) limits the scope of a variable to the enclosing blocks or file. A variable name without my keyword creates a global variable which should be avoided. In this program two variables with the same name but different cases (small and capital) are assigned values. The values of these variables are printed through print statement. Despite of the fact that both variables have the same name Perl treats them differently due to their lower and uppercase.

- It is a good practice to use the appropriate variable name according to the data to be stored in a variable. $Rbcl_gene is suitable variable name to store the gene sequence of rubisco enzyme.
- Perl does not have any problem in recognizing $string, @string and %string as scalar, array and associative array, respectively. However to avoid any confusion one should avoid the same variable name for different type of variables.
- If nothing is assigned to a variable it contains an undefined value.
- The defined values of a variable correspond to some string or number. The number 0 (zero) itself is a defined value.
- In a print statement Perl tries to interpret value of a variable when used within double quotes ("""). When single quotes '' are used it treats it as a string.

Program 2.2
Program to show interpolation
use strict;
use warnings;

my $string = 'ATGCTGCA';
my $number = 2;
print '$string and $number';
print "\n$string and $number"; # \n used for new line

Output:
$string and $number
ATGCTGCA and 2

Scalar variable

A scalar variable can hold numbers, characters or alphanumeric characters. A complete chromosome sequence can easily be stored in a scalar variable.

Program 2.3
Program to assign values to scalar variable
use strict;
use warnings;

my $number = 4321; #First variable
my $gene_seq = "ATGCTGCAGCTAGGCATGCTAGC" ; #Second variable
my $accession_number = "NC_43210" ; #Third variable

print "$number \n$gene_seq \n$accession_number";

Output:
4321
ATGCTGCAGCTAGGCATGCTAGC
NC_43210

Various formatting characters have been used in Perl with \ (backslash) symbol.

Formatting character	Description
\n	New line
\t	Tab
\u	Uppercase next character
\U	Uppercase entire line
\l	Lowercase next character
\L	Lowercase entire line
\E	End the effect of Uppercase and Lowercase

Program 2.4

```
# Program to use \n and \t
use strict;
use warnings;

my $str = 'Bio';
my $string = 'Informatics';
print "$str \n $string\n";
print "$str \t $string\n";
print "$str$string";
```

Output:

Bio

 Informatics

Bio   Informatics

BioInformatics

Program 2.5

```
# Program to convert characters in uppercase
use strict;
use warnings;
```

```perl
my $string = "biology";
print "First letter in uppercase: \u$string\n";
print "All letters in uppercase: \U$string\n";

print "Selected letters in uppercase: atgc\Utataat\Egcatcgat\n";
print "All letters in uppercase: \Uatgctataatgcatcgat\n";
```

Output:

First letter in uppercase: Biology
All letters in uppercase: BIOLOGY
Selected letters in uppercase: atgcTATAATgcatcgat
All letters in uppercase: ATGCTATAATGCATCGAT

Program 2.6

```perl
# Program to convert characters in lowercase
use strict;
use warnings;

my $string = "BIOLOGY";
print "First letter in lowercase: \l$string\n";
print "All letters in lowercase: \L$string\n";
$string = "ATGC\LTATAAT\EGCATCGAT";
print "Selected letters in lowercase: $string\n";
print "All letters in lowercase: \L$string\n";
```

Output:
First letter in lowercase: bIOLOGY
All letters in lowercase: biology
Selected letters in lowercase: ATGCtataatGCATCGAT
All letters in lowercase: atgctataatgcatcgat

Points to remember

- Always prefix the symbol used to define a variable along with variable name.
- A $ sign is prefixed with variable name to declare a scalar variable.

- @ and % sign is used to declare an array and associative array, respectively.
- When trying to print the value of a variable do not forget to prefix the symbol for variable type.
- Use formatting characters to make the output more readable.

Test Yourself

1. Write a program to assign a number to a scalar variable.
2. Write a program to store a protein sequence in a variable.
3. Write a program to print a gene sequence.
4. Write a program to store gene identifier in a variable.

Find errors

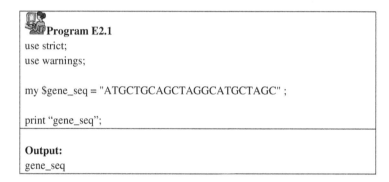

Program E2.1

```
use strict;
use warnings;

my $gene_seq = "ATGCTGCAGCTAGGCATGCTAGC" ;

print "gene_seq";
```

Output:
gene_seq

Program E2.2

```
use strict;
use warnings;

my $accession_number = "NC_43210"

print "$accession_number";
```

Output:
Error message

25

Chapter 3

Arithmetic Operations and Standard Input

Arithmetic operations can be performed on scalar variables using arithmetic operators.

Operator	Symbol
Addition	+
Subtraction	-
Multiply	*
Division	/
Remainder	%
Exponent	**
Autoincrement	++
Autodecrement	--
Add assign	+=
Subtract assign	-=

Program 3.1

```perl
# Program to add numbers
use strict;
use warnings;
```

```
my $first_number = 4;
my $second_number = 4;
my $sum = $first_number + $second_number; # 4 + 4
print "$sum";
```

Output:
8

Program 3.2
```
# Program to subtract numbers
use strict;
use warnings;

my $first_number = 4;
my $second_number = 2;
my $sub = $first_number - $second_number; # 4-2
print "$sub";
```

Output:
2

Program 3.3
```
# Program to multiply numbers
use strict;
use warnings;

my $first_number = 4;
my $second_number = 4;
my $mul = $first_number * $second_number; # 4 * 4
print "$mul";
```

Output:
16

Program 3.4
```
# Program for division
use strict;
use warnings;

my $numerator = 12;
my $denominator = 4;
my $div = $numerator / $denominator; # 12/4
print "$div";
```

Output:
```
3
```

Program 3.5
```
# Program to get remainder of division
use strict;
use warnings;

my $numerator = 8;
my $denominator = 5;
my $remainder = $numerator % $denominator; # 8/5
print "$remainder";
```

Output:
```
3
```

Program 3.6
```
# Program to get exponent
use strict;
use warnings;

my $number = 4;
my $power = 2;
my $exponent = $number ** $power; # 4²
print "$exponent";
```

Output:
16

Program 3.7
```perl
# Program to autoincrement a number
use strict;
use warnings;

my $number  = 7;
print "$number \n";
$number ++;
print "$number \n";
$number  = $number  + 1;
print "$number \n";
$number  += 1;
print "$number \n";
```

Output:
7
8
9
10

Program 3.8
```perl
# Program to autodecrement a number
use strict;
use warnings;

$number  = 7;
$number --;
print "$number \n";
$number  = $number  - 1;
print "$number \n";
$number  -= 1;
print "$number \n";
```

Output:
6

```
5
4
```

Program 3.9
```
# Program for addition and assignment
use strict;
use warnings;

my $number = 6;
$number = $number + 1;
print "$number\n";
$number += 1;
print "$number\n";
$number += 8; # $number = $number + 8;
print "$number";
```

Output:
```
7
8
16
```

Program 3.10
```
# Program for subtraction and assignment
use strict;
use warnings;

my $number = 6;
$number = $number - 1;
print "$number\n";
$number -= 1;
print "$number\n";
$number -= 3; # $number = $number - 3;
print "$number";
```

Output:
```
5
4
1
```

Instead of providing values to a variable directly in a program, values can also be assigned to a variable by taking input from keyboard during program execution.

Program 3.11

```
# Program to get input using keyboard
use strict;
use warnings;

my $first_number = <stdin>;
my $second_number = 4;
my $sum = $first_number + $second_number;
print "$sum";
```

Output:

6
10

Explanation: When execution of this program starts by typing perl programName.pl and pressing enter on command prompt the cursor starts blinking and nothing happens. The cursor blinks due to <stdin> in the program where it asks for input through keyboard. If the input is not provided it will not move to the next statement for execution. Here the number 6 is provided using keyboard. As soon as the enter key is pressed the other statements get executed and another number 10 appears in the output which is the sum of 6 + 4.

It is a good practice to write interactive programs. The above program is not interactive. As the execution starts the cursor blinks without any message on the screen. May be the user entered a character instead of a number that is what user does not intend to do, by adding a character and a number.

Program 3.12
Program to get input using keyboard in interactive manner
use strict;
use warnings;

print "Enter first number = ";
my $first_number = <stdin>;

print "Enter second number = ";
my $second_number = <stdin>;

my $sum = $first_number + $second_number;
print "The sum of numbers is = $sum";

Output:
Enter first number = 4
Enter second number = 6
The sum of numbers is = 10

The value entered using keyboard can be seen by using print statement with desired variable name.

Program 3.13
Program to get input using keyboard and display the entered value
use strict;
use warnings;

print "Enter first number = ";
my $first_number = <stdin>;
print "First number is = $first_number";

print "Enter second number = ";
my $second_number = <stdin>;
print "Second number is = $second_number";

my $sum = $first_number + $second_number;
print "The sum of numbers is = $sum";

Output:
Enter first number = 6

```
First number is = 6
Enter second number = 4
Second number is = 4
The sum of numbers is = 10
```

Notice here that a new line character ("\n") is not used in print statements however still the output appears in new lines. This is due to the presence of new line character along with the number entered from keyboard. When value has been entered from the keyboard the new line character which is a hidden character appended with the value. When arithmetic operations have been done it does not have any effect on them. However a simple print statement with two values taken from keyboard shows that hidden new line character.

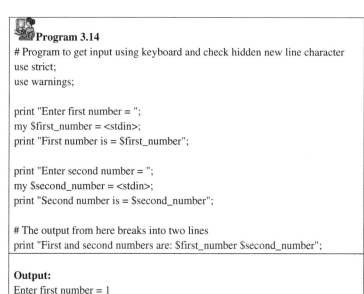

Program 3.14

```perl
# Program to get input using keyboard and check hidden new line character
use strict;
use warnings;

print "Enter first number = ";
my $first_number = <stdin>;
print "First number is = $first_number";

print "Enter second number = ";
my $second_number = <stdin>;
print "Second number is = $second_number";

# The output from here breaks into two lines
print "First and second numbers are: $first_number $second_number";
```

Output:
```
Enter first number = 1
First number is = 1
Enter second number = 2
Second number is = 2
First and second numbers are: 1
2
```

To remove hidden new line character chomp function is used.

Program 3.15
```perl
# Program to get input using keyboard and remove new line character
use strict;
use warnings;

print "Enter first number = ";
my $first_number = <stdin>;
print "First number is = $first_number";

print "Enter second number = ";
my $second_number = <stdin>;
print "Second number is = $second_number";
# The output from here breaks into two lines
print "First and second numbers are: $first_number $second_number";

chomp ($first_number) ;
chomp ($second_number) ;

print "In a single line: $first_number * $second_number";
```

Output:
```
Enter first number = 1
First number is = 1
Enter second number = 2
Second number is = 2
First and second numbers are: 1
 2
In a single line: 1 * 2
```

Explanation: The new line character appended at the end of value entered through keyboard has been removed by chomp function. Therefore the output finally appears in a single line.

Program 3.16
```perl
# Program to get strings from keyboard
use strict;
use warnings;
```

34

```
print "Enter first string = ";
my $first_string = <stdin>;
print "First string is = $first_string";

print "Enter second string = ";
my $second_string = <stdin>;
print "Second string is = $second_string";

print "Strings entered are: ";
print "$first_string $second_string";

#Remove new line character appended at the end
chomp ($first_string) ;

print "Strings entered after applying chomp: ";
print "$first_string$second_string";
```

Output:
Enter first string = Bio
First string is = Bio
Enter second string = Informatics
Second string is = Informatics
Strings entered are: Bio
 Informatics
Strings entered after applying chomp: BioInformatics

Another function named chop can also be used to remove new line character, but chop can remove any character from the end.

Program 3.17
```
# Program to get strings from keyboard and remove new line using chop
use strict;
use warnings;

print "Enter first string = ";
my $first_string = <stdin>;
print "First string is = $first_string";

print "Enter second string = ";
my $second_string = <stdin>;
print "Second string is = $second_string";
```

```
print "Strings entered are: ";
print "$first_string $second_string";

#Remove new line character appended at the end
chop ($first_string) ;

print "Strings entered after applying chop: ";
print "$first_string$second_string";
```

Output:
Enter first string = Bio
First string is = Bio
Enter second string = Informatics
Second string is = Informatics
Strings entered are: Bio
 Informatics
Strings entered after applying chop: BioInformatics

The effect of chop and chomp can be easily seen by applying these functions on a string.

Program 3.18
```
# Program to check the effect of chomp on a string
use strict;
use warnings;

my $string = 'BioInformatics';
print "String: $string\n";
chomp($string);
print "After chomp: $string\n";
```

Output:
String: BioInformatics
After chomp: BioInformatics

Explanation: Since chomp function specifically works on new line character therefore it does not have any effect on the string.

Program 3.19

```perl
# Program to check the effect of chop on a string
use strict;
use warnings;

my $string = 'BioInformatics';
print "String: $string\n";
chop($string);
print "After chop: $string\n";
chop($string);
print "After chop: $string\n";
chop($string);
print "After chop: $string\n";
chop($string);
print "After chop: $string\n";
chop($string);
print "After chop: $string\n";
chop($string);
print "After chop: $string\n";
chop($string);
print "After chop: $string\n";
chop($string);
print "After chop: $string\n";
chop($string);
print "After chop: $string\n";
chop($string);
print "After chop: $string\n";
chop($string);
print "After chop: $string\n";
```

Output:

String: BioInformatics

After chop: BioInformatic

After chop: BioInformati

After chop: BioInformat

After chop: BioInforma

After chop: BioInform

After chop: BioInfor

After chop: BioInfo

After chop: BioInf
After chop: BioIn
After chop: BioI
After chop: Bio

Explanation: Chop function can happily cut any character from end.

Points to remember

- Use chomp function to remove new line character.
- The chop function cut any character from end of scalar, array and associative array.
- The symbol % is used to get the remainder of a division.
- Double stars (**) are used to get the exponent.
- During program execution <stdin> helps to take input.

Test Yourself

1. Write a program to add five numbers.
2. Write a program to get remainder of division.
3. Write a program to print a table of 2.
4. Write a program to calculate percentage of a student.

Find errors

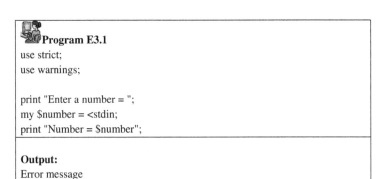

Program E3.1
```
use strict;
use warnings;

print "Enter a number = ";
my $number = <stdin;
print "Number = $number";
```

Output:
Error message

Program E3.2

```
use strict;
#use warnings;

print "Enter first number = ";
my $first_number = <stdin>;
chop($first_number);
print "Enter second number = ";
my $second_number = <stdin>;
chop($first_number);
my $sum = $first_number + $second_number;
print "The sum of numbers is = $sum";
```

Output:
Enter first number = 4
Enter second number = 4
The sum of numbers is = 4

Chapter 4

Arrays

An array is a collection of multiple scalar values, also known as array elements, stored in an ordered manner. These values are numbers, strings or combination of both. Each value is associated with an index number using which the values stored in an array can be accessed. The index number of an array always starts with 0.

	Value 1	Value 2	Value 3	Value 4
@array =	Gene1	Gene2	Gene3	Gene4
	Index 0	Index 1	Index 2	Index 3

Program 4.1

```
# Program to create an array of strings
use strict;
use warnings;

#array of strings
my @array = ('A', 'book', 'on', 'Perl');
print "Array of strings\n";
print "@array","\n";
```

Output:
```
Array of strings
A book on Perl
```

Array is an ordered list therefore 'A' stores in 0th index of array, 'book' stores in 1st index of array and so on.

	Value 1	Value 2	Value 3	Value 4
@array =	A	book	on	Perl
	Index 0	Index 1	Index 2	Index 3

Program 4.2
Program to create an array of numbers
use strict;
use warnings;

#array of numbers
my @array = (12, 3, 1, 7, 2);
print "Array of numbers\n";
print "@array","\n";

Output:
Array of numbers
12 3 1 7 2

Being an ordered list the @array stores 12 in 0th index, 3 in 1st index and so on.

Program 4.3
Program to create an array of strings and numbers
use strict;
use warnings;

#array of strings and numbers
my @array = ('Year', 2014);
print "Array of strings and numbers\n";
print "@array","\n";

Output:
Array of strings and numbers
Year 2014

Program 4.4
Program to assign array using quote word function
use strict;
use warnings;

my @array = qw (a b c d e);
print "Print without double quotes\n";
print @**array**,"\n\n";
print "Print with double quotes\n";
print "@array","\n";

Output:
Print without double quotes
abcde
Print with double quotes
a b c d e

Notice the difference while printing the values of an array with or without quotes. Without quotes all the values from different indexes of an array appear with no space between them while when an array is enclosed within double quotes the values from different index will appear with some space between them. The second method is the cleaner method to print array values.

Program 4.5
Program to use quote word function in interpolation mode
use strict;
use warnings;

my $var = 'e';
my @array = qw (a b c d $**var**);
print "qw does not works in interpolation mode\n";
print "@array","\n";

Output:
qw does not works in interpolation mode
a b c d $**var**

Program 4.6

```
# Program to assign array using scalar variables
use strict;
use warnings;

#assign array using scalar variables
my $gene = 'ATAGCAGGCTAGT';
my $protein = 'MASDGHYTWR';
my $rna = 'CAGUCAUCU';

my @array = ("$gene","$rna","$protein");
print "@array","\n";

@array = ('$gene',"$rna",$protein);
print "@array","\n";
```

Output:
ATAGCAGGCTAGT CAGUCAUCU MASDGHYTWR
$gene CAGUCAUCU MASDGHYTWR

Notice the single quote on '**$gene**', it will treat this as a string therefore the same will appear in output without interpolation.

Program 4.7

```
# Program to assign one array to another array
use strict;
use warnings;

#assign array
my @array = (12,3,1,7,2);
print "Array\n";
print "@array","\n\n";
#assign array to another array
my @new_array = @array;
print "New array\n";
print "@new_array","\n";
```

Output:
Array
1 2 3 1 7 2

New array
1 2 3 1 7 2

Program 4.8

```
# Program to merge multiple array into one array
use strict;
use warnings;

my @array = (20,30,10,70);
my @array_string = ('One', 'Two');
my @new_array = (2,3,1,7);

#assign multiple arrays to an array
my @array_merge = (@new_array, @array_string, @array);

print "Multiple array merged\n";
print "@array_merge","\n";
```

Output:

Multiple array merged
2 3 1 7 One Two 20 30 10 70

Notice that the values of different arrays are merged in the same order as arrays are provided.

Program 4.9

```
# Program to assign values to specific index of an array
use strict;
use warnings;

#Array declaration
my @genes = (); #Creates an empty array
print "@genes\t########\n";
```

```
#Assign value to 0th index
$genes[0] = 'MDR1';

#Assign value to 1st index
$genes[1] = 'BRAC2';

print "Print array\n";
print "@genes","\n\n";

print "Print value of 0th index\n";
print "$genes[0]\n";
```

Output:
```
########
Print array
MDR1 BRAC2

Print value of 0th index
MDR1
```

Notice that when the empty array is printed nothing appears in the output.

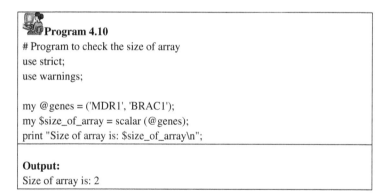

Program 4.10
```
# Program to check the size of array
use strict;
use warnings;

my @genes = ('MDR1', 'BRAC1');
my $size_of_array = scalar (@genes);
print "Size of array is: $size_of_array\n";
```

Output:
```
Size of array is: 2
```

The size of array equals the number of elements present in it. Since there are two elements assigned to array therefore the size of array is 2.

Program 4.11

```
# Program to empty an array
use strict;
use warnings;

my @genes = ('MDR1', 'BRAC1');
my $size_of_array = scalar (@genes);
print "Size of array is: $size_of_array\n";
@genes = ();
$size_of_array = scalar (@genes);
print "Size of empty array: $size_of_array\n";
```

Output:
Size of array is: 2
Size of empty array: 0

Program 4.12

```
# Program to check the size of array without scalar function
use strict;
use warnings;

my @genes = ('MDR1', 'BRAC1');
my $size_of_array = @genes;
print "Size of array is: $size_of_array\n";
```

Output:
Size of array is: 2

Program 4.13

```
# Program to check the last index of array
use strict;
use warnings;

my @genes = ('MDR1', 'BRAC1');
my $last_index_of_array = $#genes;
```

```
print "Last index of array is: $last_index_of_array\n";
```

Output:
Last index of array is: 1

Since index of an array always starts with 0, therefore the last index of an array is always one less than its size. If there are 2 values stored in an array its last index will be 1. The size of array can also be checked by adding 1 to last index. Similarly the last index of an array can be determined by subtracting 1 from array size.

Program 4.14

```
# Program to check the size of array using last index
use strict;
use warnings;

my @genes = ('MDR1', 'BRAC1');
my $size_of_array = $#genes+1;
print "Size of array is: $size_of_array\n";
```

Output:
Size of array is: 2

Program 4.15

```
# Program to check the last index of array using array size
use strict;
use warnings;

my @genes = ('MDR1', 'BRAC1');
my $last_index_of_array = @genes-1;
print "Last index of array is: $last_index_of_array\n";
```

Output:

Last index of array is: 1

Program 4.16

\# Program to print value stored in last index of array
use strict;
use warnings;

my @genes = ('MDR1', 'BRAC1');
print "$genes[$#genes]\n";

Output:

BRAC1

Following functions are used to manipulate an array:

Function	Description
Push	Add element at end of array
Pop	Remove element from end of array
Unshift	Add element at beginning of array
Shift	Remove element from beginning of array
Splice	Add/ Remove element in between of array
Reverse	Reverse the array
Sort	Sort the array
Join	Join elements of array

Program 4.17

\# Program to add array element at the end

use strict;

use warnings;

```
my @genes = ('MDR1', 'BRAC1');
print "Elements in array: @genes","\n";
push (@genes, 'RBCL');
print "Elements in array after manipulation: @genes","\n";
```

Output:

Elements in array: MDR1 BRAC1

Elements in array after manipulation: MDR1 BRAC1 RBCL

Program 4.18

```
# Program to remove array element from end
use strict;
use warnings;

my @genes = ('MDR1', 'BRAC1');
print "Elements in array: @genes","\n";
pop (@genes);
print "Elements in array after manipulation: @genes","\n";
```

Output:
Elements in array: MDR1 BRAC1
Elements in array after manipulation: MDR1

Pop can return the value that it cuts from end.

Program 4.19

```
# Program to remove array element from end and print the value
use strict;
use warnings;

my @genes = ('MDR1', 'BRAC1');
print "Elements in array: @genes","\n";
my $last_element = pop (@genes);
print "Elements in array after manipulation: @genes","\n";
print "Last element of array removed by pop function is: $last_element","\n";
```

Output:
Elements in array: MDR1 BRAC1
Elements in array after manipulation: MDR1
Last element of array removed by pop function is: BRAC1

Program 4.20

```
# Program to add array element in the beginning
use strict;
use warnings;

my @genes = ('MDR1', 'BRAC1');
print "Elements in array: @genes","\n";
unshift (@genes, 'RBCL');
print "Elements in array after manipulation: @genes","\n";
```

Output:
Elements in array: MDR1 BRAC1
Elements in array after manipulation: RBCL MDR1 BRAC1

Program 4.21

```
# Program to remove array element from beginning
use strict;
use warnings;

my @genes = ('MDR1', 'BRAC1');
print "Elements in array: @genes","\n";
shift (@genes);
print "Elements in array after manipulation: @genes","\n";
```

Output:
Elements in array: MDR1 BRAC1
Elements in array after manipulation: BRAC1

Program 4.22

```
# Program to remove array element from beginning and print the value
use strict;
use warnings;

my @genes = ('MDR1', 'BRAC1');
print "Elements in array: @genes","\n";
my $first_element = shift (@genes);
print "Elements in array after manipulation: @genes","\n";
print "First element of array removed by shift function is: $first_element","\n";
```

Output:
Elements in array: MDR1 BRAC1
Elements in array after manipulation: BRAC1
First element of array removed by shift function is: MDR1

Array manipulation can change the size of array. Since array indexes always start with 0, therefore automatic adjustment of array indexes occurs after every manipulation (addition or removal) event.

Program 4.23

```
# Program to remove array element from beginning and add it at the end
use strict;
use warnings;

# Program to remove array element from beginning and add it at the end
my @genes = ('MDR1', 'BRAC1', 'RBCL');
print "Elements in array: @genes","\n";
my $first_element = shift (@genes);
print "Elements in array after shift: @genes","\n";
print "First element of array removed by shift function is: $first_element","\n";
push (@genes,"$first_element");
print "Elements in array after push: @genes","\n";
```

Output:
Elements in array: MDR1 BRAC1 RBCL
Elements in array after shift: BRAC1 RBCL
First element of array removed by shift function is: MDR1
Elements in array after push: BRAC1 RBCL MDR1

Program 4.24
```
# Program to check the size of array after array manipulation
use strict;
use warnings;

my @genes = ('MDR1', 'BRAC1', 'RBCL');
print "Elements in array: @genes","\n";
my $size_of_array = scalar (@genes);
print "Size of array is: $size_of_array\n";
my $first_element = shift (@genes);
print "Elements in array after shift: @genes","\n";
print "First element of array removed by shift function is: $first_element","\n";
$size_of_array = scalar (@genes);
print "Size of array after shift: $size_of_array\n";
push (@genes,"$first_element");
print "Elements in array after push: @genes","\n";
$size_of_array = scalar (@genes);
print "Size of array after push: $size_of_array\n";
```

Output:
```
Elements in array: MDR1 BRAC1 RBCL
Size of array is: 3
Elements in array after shift: BRAC1 RBCL
First element of array removed by shift function is: MDR1
Size of array after shift: 2
Elements in array after push: BRAC1 RBCL MDR1
Size of array after push: 3
```

Program 4.25
```
# Program to check the last index of array after array manipulation
use strict;
use warnings;

my @genes = ('MDR1', 'BRAC1', 'RBCL');
print "Elements in array: @genes","\n";
my $last_index_of_array = $#genes;
print "Last index of array is: $last_index_of_array\n";
```

```
my $first_element = shift (@genes);
print "Elements in array after shift: @genes","\n";
print "First element of array removed by shift function is: $first_element","\n";
$last_index_of_array = $#genes;
print "Last index of array after shift: $last_index_of_array\n";
push (@genes,"$first_element");
print "Elements in array after push: @genes","\n";
$last_index_of_array = $#genes;
print "Last index of array after push: $last_index_of_array\n";
```

Output:
Elements in array: MDR1 BRAC1 RBCL
Last index of array is: 2
Elements in array after shift: BRAC1 RBCL
First element of array removed by shift function is: MDR1
Last index of array after shift: 1
Elements in array after push: BRAC1 RBCL MDR1
Last index of array after push: 2

Splice (Array, Offset, Length, List);

Array = Name of array

Offset = Index number from where manipulation required

Length = Total indexes to be manipulated including offset

List = Elements to add in array

Program 4.26
```
# Program to insert elements in-between array indexes
# by replacing other elements
use strict;
use warnings;

my @array = qw (gene1 gene2 gene3 gene4 gene5 gene6);
print "Elements in array: @array","\n";
splice (@array, 2, 3, 'gene7');
print "Elements in array: @array","\n";
```

Output:
Elements in array: gene1 gene2 **gene3 gene4 gene5** gene6
Elements in array: gene1 gene2 **gene7** gene6

Here the splice function starts from 2nd index with array element gene3 and removes elements from indexes 2, 3 and 4. Finally it inserts the array element gene7 at 2nd index of array.

Program 4.27

```
# Program to insert elements in-between array indexes
# without replacing other elements
use strict;
use warnings;

my @array = qw (gene1 gene2 gene3 gene4 gene5 gene6);
print "Elements in array: @array","\n";
splice (@array,2,0, 'gene7', 'gene8');
print "Elements in array: @array","\n";
```

Output:

Elements in array: gene1 gene2 gene3 gene4 gene5 gene6

Elements in array: gene1 gene2 **gene7 gene8** gene3 gene4 gene5 gene6

Here 0 in the splice function ensures that only addition of new elements occurs.

Program 4.28

```
# Program to remove element from in-between array indexes
# without adding new elements
use strict;
use warnings;

my @array = qw (gene1 gene2 gene3 gene4 gene5 gene6);
print "Elements in array: @array","\n";
splice (@array,2,1);
print "Elements in array: @array","\n";
```

Output:

Elements in array: gene1 gene2 gene3 gene4 gene5 gene6

Elements in array: gene1 gene2 gene4 gene5 gene6

Since the list is not provided in the splice function which ensures that only removal of array element at 2nd index occurs, because the length is taken as 1, with no element insertion.

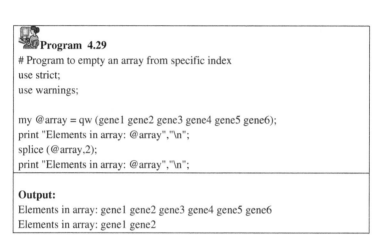

Program 4.29
Program to empty an array from specific index
use strict;
use warnings;

my @array = qw (gene1 gene2 gene3 gene4 gene5 gene6);
print "Elements in array: @array","\n";
splice (@array,2);
print "Elements in array: @array","\n";

Output:
Elements in array: gene1 gene2 gene3 gene4 gene5 gene6
Elements in array: gene1 gene2

All indexes have been deleted starting from index 2. Notice that the memory occupied by these indexes has been freed.

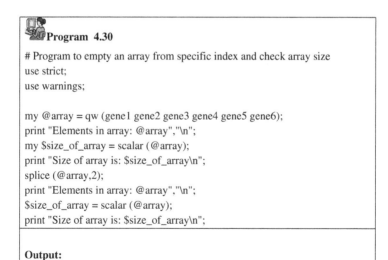

Program 4.30

Program to empty an array from specific index and check array size
use strict;
use warnings;

my @array = qw (gene1 gene2 gene3 gene4 gene5 gene6);
print "Elements in array: @array","\n";
my $size_of_array = scalar (@array);
print "Size of array is: $size_of_array\n";
splice (@array,2);
print "Elements in array: @array","\n";
$size_of_array = scalar (@array);
print "Size of array is: $size_of_array\n";

Output:

Elements in array: gene1 gene2 gene3 gene4 gene5 gene6

Size of array is: 6
Elements in array: gene1 gene2
Size of array is: 2

Program 4.31

Program to reverse array
use strict;
use warnings;
@array = qw (gene1 gene2 gene3 gene4 gene5 gene6);
print "Elements in array: @array","\n";
my @reverse_array = reverse (@array);
print "Elements in reverse order: @reverse_array","\n";

Output:
Elements in array: gene1 gene2 gene3 gene4 gene5 gene6
Elements in reverse order: gene6 gene5 gene4 gene3 gene2 gene1

Program 4.32

Program to sort array
use strict;
use warnings;

my @array = qw (gene6 gene5 gene3 gene1 gene2 gene4);
print "Elements in array: @array","\n";
my @sorted_array = sort (@array);
print "Sorted array: @sorted_array","\n";

Output:
Elements in array: gene6 gene5 gene3 gene1 gene2 gene4
Sorted array: gene1 gene2 gene3 gene4 gene5 gene6

Program 4.33

```perl
# Program to join array elements
use strict;
use warnings;

my @array = qw (gene1 gene2 gene3 gene4 gene5 gene6);
print "Elements in array: @array","\n";
print "Joined array using , :", join (', ',@array) ,"\n";
print "Joined array using # :", join ('#',@array) ,"\n";
```

Output:

Elements in array: gene1 gene2 gene3 gene4 gene5 gene6
Joined array using , :gene1,gene2,gene3,gene4,gene5,gene6
Joined array using # :gene1#gene2#gene3#gene4#gene5#gene6

Program 4.34

```perl
# Program to check the effect of chop on array
use strict;
use warnings;

my @array = qw (AB BC CD DE EF);
print "Array: @array\n";
chop(@array);
print "After chop: @array\n";
```

Output:
Array: AB BC CD DE EF
After chop: A B C D E

Explanation: Chop function cuts any character from end in the values stored in each index of array.

Points to remember

- A @ sign is prefixed with variable name to declare an array.
- Array index always starts with 0.
- The functions push and pop are used to manipulate array from end.

- Shift and unshift are used to manipulate array from beginning.
- Splice can manipulate array in between indexes.

Test Yourself

1. Write a program to swap values in 0th and last index of array.

2. Write a program to remove the value from 2nd index of array.

3. Write a program to know the last index of array.

4. Write a program to reverse the array values.

Find errors

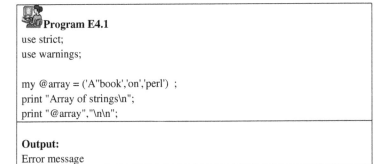

Program E4.1
use strict;
use warnings;

my @array = ('A"book','on','perl') ;
print "Array of strings\n";
print "@array","\n\n";

Output:
Error message

Program E4.2
use strict;
use warnings;

my @genes = ('MDR1', 'BRAC1') ;
print "Value in last index: $genes[#genes]\n";

Output:
Error message

Chapter 5

Associative Arrays

An associative array also holds multiple scalar values but in an unordered manner. Each value is associated with a key (just like index in an array) which is usually a string. Therefore there is always a key-value pair in associative array. In a print statement an associative array appears in the form of key-value pairs. However the order of each key-value pair is usually not exactly the same as provided while assigning the associative array.

%hash =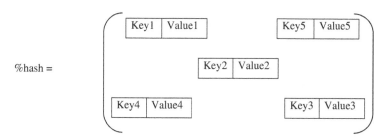

Program 5.1
```
# Program to create associative array
use strict;
use warnings;

#%Gene_length = ('Key1',value1, 'Key2',value2, 'Key3',value3);
my %Gene_length = ('MDR', 2400, 'BRAC', 2267, 'Rubisco', 1700);
print "Key-value pairs in associative array: ",%Gene_length,"\n";
```

#Another way to assign associative array
my %Gene_length_again = ('MDR' => 2400, 'BRAC' => 2267, 'Rubisco' => 1700);
print "Key-value pairs in associative array: ",%Gene_length_again,"\n";

Output:
Key-value pairs in associative array: **Rubisco1700BRAC2267MDR2400**
Key-value pairs in associative array: **MDR2400BRAC2267Rubisco1700**

Notice the order of key-value pair in the output. This is due to unordered nature of associative array. Moreover in the print statement the variable name for associative array is not enclosed in double quotes. In between double quotes the associative array act as a string.

Program 5.2
Program to check effect of double quotes on associative array
use strict;
use warnings;

my %Gene_length = ('MDR', 2400, 'BRAC', 2267, 'Rubisco', 1700);
print "Within quotes: %Gene_length\n";
print "Without quotes:", %Gene_length,"\n";

Output:
Within quotes: **%Gene_length**
Without quotes: MDR2400BRAC2267Rubisco1700

Program 5.3
Program to assign value to a specific key
use strict;
use warnings;

my %Gene_length = ('MDR', 2400, 'BRAC', 2267, 'Rubisco', 1700);
print "Key-value pairs in associative array: ",%Gene_length,"\n";
#$Gene_length{'Key'} = value;
$Gene_length{'matK'} = 1800;
print "Key-value pairs after adding new key-value: ",%Gene_length,"\n";

Output:
Key-value pairs in associative array: Rubisco1700MDR2400BRAC2267
Key-value   pairs   after   adding   new   key-value   pair:
matK1800MDR2400Rubisco1700BRAC2267

Program 5.4

```perl
# Program to print value of a key
use strict;
use warnings;

my %Gene_length = ('MDR', 2400, 'BRAC', 2267, 'Rubisco', 1700);
print "Key-value pairs in associative array: ",%Gene_length,"\n";
print "Value associated with key MDR is: $Gene_length{'MDR'} \n";
```

Output:

Key-value pairs in associative array: BRAC2267MDR2400Rubisco1700

Value associated with key MDR is: 2400

Following functions are specific to associative array:

Function	Description
keys	Retrieve all keys of associative array
values	Retrieve all values of associative array
each	Retrieve key-value pair of associative array
delete	Delete key-value pair of associative array

Program 5.5

```perl
# Program to retrieve keys
use strict;
use warnings;

my %Gene_length = ('MDR', 2400, 'BRAC', 2267, 'Rubisco', 1700);
print "Key-value pairs in associative array: ",%Gene_length,"\n";
```

```
my @key = keys (%Gene_length);
print "Keys in %Gene_length associative array are: @key","\n";
```

Output:
Key-value pairs in associative array: BRAC2267MDR2400Rubisco1700
Keys in %Gene_length associative array are: BRAC MDR Rubisco

Program 5.6

```
# Program to retrieve values
use strict;
use warnings;

my %Gene_length = ('MDR', 2400, 'BRAC', 2267, 'Rubisco', 1700);
print "Key-value pairs in associative array: ",%Gene_length,"\n";
my @value = values (%Gene_length);
print "Values in %Gene_length associative array are: @value","\n";
```

Output:

Key-value pairs in associative array: MDR2400Rubisco1700BRAC2267

Values in %Gene_length associative array are: 2400 1700 2267

Program 5.7

```
# Program to empty associative array
use strict;
use warnings;

my %Gene_length = ('MDR', 2400, 'BRAC', 2267, 'Rubisco', 1700);
print "Key-value pairs in associative array: ",%Gene_length,"\n";
%Gene_length = ();
print "Empty hash", %Gene_length,"\n";
```

Output:

Key-value pairs in associative array: Rubisco1700MDR2400BRAC2267

Empty hash

Program 5.8

```
# Program to undefine a value associated with a key
use strict;
use warnings;

my %Gene_length = ('MDR', 2400, 'BRAC', 2267, 'Rubisco', 1700);
print "Key-value pairs in associative array: ",%Gene_length,"\n";
undef ($Gene_length{'Rubisco'});
print "Key-value pairs in associative array: ",%Gene_length,"\n";
```

Output:
Key-value pairs in associative array: BRAC2267**Rubisco1700**MDR2400
Key-value pairs in associative array: BRAC2267**Rubisco**MDR2400

Program 5.9

```
# Program to delete a key-value pair
use strict;
use warnings;

my %Gene_length = ('MDR', 2400, 'BRAC', 2267, 'Rubisco', 1700);
print "Key-value pairs in associative array: ",%Gene_length,"\n";
delete ($Gene_length{'Rubisco'});
print "Key-value pairs in associative array: ",%Gene_length,"\n";
```

Output:
Key-value pairs in associative array: BRAC2267**Rubisco1700**MDR2400
Key-value pairs in associative array: BRAC2267MDR2400

Program 5.10
```
# Program to check the effect of chop on associative array
use strict;
use warnings;

my %Gene_length = ( 'MDR', 2400,'BRAC', 2267,'Rubisco', 1700)  ;
print "Key-value pairs in associative array: ",%Gene_length,"\n";
chop(%Gene_length);
print "After chop: \n\n";

print "MDR => $Gene_length{'MDR'}\n";
print "BRAC => $Gene_length{'BRAC'}\n";
print "Rubisco => $Gene_length{'Rubisco'}\n";
```

Output:
Key-value pairs in associative array: Rubisco1700MDR2400BRAC2267
After chop:

MDR => 240
BRAC => 226
Rubisco => 170

Explanation: Chop function cuts any character from end in the values associated with each key of associative array.

Points to remember

- A % sign is prefixed with variable name to declare an associative array.
- Associative array is an unordered list.
- Each key is associated with a value.

Test Yourself

1. Write a program to retrieve keys of associative array.
2. Write a program to undefine a value associated with a key.
3. Write a program to count number of keys present in associative array.
4. Write a program to delete a key-value pair from associative array.

Find errors

Program E5.1

use strict;
use warnings;

my %Gene_length = ('MDR' = 2400,'BRAC' = 2267,'Rubisco' = 1700) ;
print "Key-value pairs in associative array: ",%Gene_length,"\n";

Output:
Error message

Program E5.2

use strict;
use warnings;

my %Gene_length = ('MDR', 2400,'BRAC', 2267,'Rubisco', 1700) ;
print "Key-value pairs in associative array: %Gene_length\n";

Output:
Key-value pairs in associative array: %Gene_length

Chapter 6

Comparison Operators and Choices

Comparison operators are used to compare strings or numeric values.

Comparison operators		
Description	**Numeric**	**String**
Equal to	==	eq
Not equal to	!=	ne
Greater than	>	gt
Greater than or equal to	>=	ge
Less than	<	lt
Less than or equal to	<=	le

Choices

Choices can be made in Perl using if statement.

```
if (expression)
{

Code block;

}
```

The code block gets executed only if the expression turns out to be true.

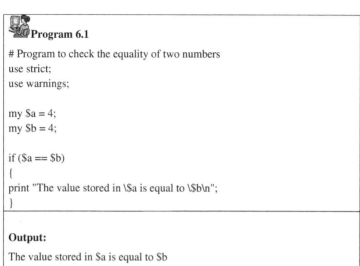

Program 6.1

```perl
# Program to check the equality of two numbers
use strict;
use warnings;

my $a = 4;
my $b = 4;

if ($a == $b)
{
print "The value stored in \$a is equal to \$b\n";
}
```

Output:

The value stored in $a is equal to $b

Notice the \ before variable name in print statement. It prints the variable itself without interpolation.

Program 6.2

```perl
# Program to check the non-equality of two numbers
use strict;
use warnings;

my $a = 4;
my $b = 8;

if ($a != $b)
{
print "The value stored in \$a is not equal to \$b\n";
}
```

Output:

The value stored in $a is not equal to $b

Program 6.3

```perl
# Program to check which number is greater
use strict;
use warnings;

my $a = 8;
my $b = 4;

if ($a > $b)
{
print "The value stored in \$a is greater than \$b\n";
}
```

Output:

The value stored in $a is greater than $b

Program 6.4

```perl
# Program to check whether number is greater than or equal
use strict;
use warnings;

my $a = 4;
my $b = 4;

if ($a >= $b)
{
print "The value stored in \$a is greater than or equal to \$b\n";
}
```

Output:

The value stored in $a is greater than or equal to $b

Program 6.5

```
# Program to check which number is lesser
use strict;
use warnings;

my $a = 4;
my $b = 8;

if ($a < $b)
{
print "The value stored in \$a is less than \$b\n";
}
```

Output:

The value stored in $a is less than $b

Program 6.6

```
# Program to check whether number is less than or equal
use strict;
use warnings;

my $a = 4;
my $b = 4;

if ($a <= $b)
{
print "The value stored in \$a is less than or equal to \$b\n";
}
```

Output:

The value stored in $a is less than or equal to $b

In case the expression turns out to be false there will be no output.

Program 6.7

Program to check the logical error
use strict;
use warnings;

my $a = 8;
my $b = 4;

if ($a < $b)
{
print "The value stored in \$a is less than \$b\n";
}

Output:

No output appears in this case since the expression is false. Therefore to deal with such cases when expression fails and user wish to print some default message if-else is used. In if-else either if or else block executes.

if (expression)
{

If code block;

}
else
{

Else code block;

}

The if code block gets executed only if the expression turns out to be true otherwise else block executes.

Program 6.8

```
# Program to use if-else
use strict;
use warnings;

my $a = 8;
my $b = 4;

if ($a < $b)
{
print "The value stored in \$a is less than \$b\n";
}
else
{
print "The value stored in \$a is greater than \$b\n";
}
```

Output:
The value stored in $a is greater than $b

To test multiple cases if-elsif-else is used.

```
if (expression)
{

If code block;

}

elsif (expression)
{

Elsif code block;

}

else
{

Else code block;
```

}

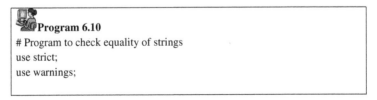

Program 6.9
```
# Program to use if-elsif-else
use strict;
use warnings;

my $a = 8;
my $b = 4;

if ($a < $b)
{
print "The value stored in \$a is less than \$b\n";
}

elsif ($a > $b)
{
print "The value stored in \$a is greater than \$b\n";
}

else
{
print "The value stored in \$a is equal to \$b\n";
}
```

Output:
The value stored in $a is greater than $b

The string comparison operators work on strings. Perl uses alphabetical position in a character table to compare the strings. The character table has a unique index for each character. During comparison these indexes have been compared to know which character is greater. Capital 'A' is greater than small 'a' which itself is less than 'z'.

Program 6.10
```
# Program to check equality of strings
use strict;
use warnings;
```

```
my $a = "Biology";
my $b = "Biology";

if ($a eq $b)
{
print "The value stored in \$a is equal to \$b\n";
}

else
{
print "The value stored in \$a is not equal to \$b\n";
}
```

Output:
The value stored in $a is equal to $b

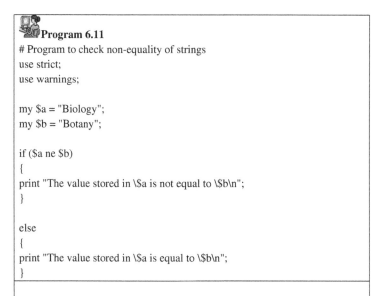

Program 6.11
```
# Program to check non-equality of strings
use strict;
use warnings;

my $a = "Biology";
my $b = "Botany";

if ($a ne $b)
{
print "The value stored in \$a is not equal to \$b\n";
}

else
{
print "The value stored in \$a is equal to \$b\n";
}
```

Output:
The value stored in $a is not equal to $b

Program 6.12

```perl
# Program to check which string is greater
use strict;
use warnings;

my $a = "Zoology";
my $b = "Botany";

if ($a gt $b)
{
print "The value stored in \$a is greater than \$b\n";
}

else
{
print "The value stored in \$a is lesser than \$b\n";
}
```

Output:
The value stored in $a is greater than $b

Program 6.13

```perl
# Program to check whether string is greater or equal
use strict;
use warnings;

my $a = "Zoology";
my $b = "Botany";

if ($a ge $b)
{
print "The value stored in \$a is greater than or equal to \$b\n";
}

else
{
print "The value stored in \$a is lesser than \$b\n";
}
```

Output:
The value stored in $a is greater than or equal to $b

Program 6.14
```perl
# Program to check which string is lesser
use strict;
use warnings;

my $a = "Botany";
my $b = "Zoology";

if ($a lt $b)
{
print "The value stored in \$a is less than \$b\n";
}

else
{
print "The value stored in \$a is greater than \$b\n";
}
```

Output:
The value stored in $a is less than $b

Program 6.15
```perl
# Program to check whether string is lesser or equal
use strict;
use warnings;

my $a = "Botany";
my $b = "Zoology";

if ($a le $b)
{
print "The value stored in \$a is less than or equal to \$b\n";
}
```

else
{
print "The value stored in \$a is greater than \$b\n";
}

Output:
The value stored in $a is less than or equal to $b

Program 6.16
Program to check whether a key in associative array contains a defined value
use strict;
use warnings;

my %Gene_length = ('MDR' => 2400, 'BRAC' => 2100, 'Rubisco' => 1800, 'Gene');

if (defined ($Gene_length{'Gene'}))
{
print "Key contains a defined value\n";
}
else
{
print "Key does not contains a defined value\n";
}

Output:
Key does not contains a defined value

Explanation: Only the key Gene is provided while assigning the associative array therefore the value corresponding to that key remains undefined. Check for any other key whose value is provided then if block executes.

The defined function returns true if the value is provided to the key and false otherwise.

Program 6.17

```perl
# Program to check defined value of a key
use strict;
use warnings;

my %Gene_length = ('MDR' => 2400, 'BRAC' => 2100, 'Rubisco' => 1800);

if (defined ($Gene_length{'MDR'}) )
{
print "Key contains a defined value\n";
}
else
{
print "Key does not contains a defined value\n";
}
```

Output:

Key contains a defined value

Program 6.18

```perl
# Program to check whether a key exists in associative array
use strict;
use warnings;

my %Gene_length = ('MDR' => 2400, 'BRAC' => 2100, 'Rubisco' => 1800, 'Gene');
if (exists ($Gene_length{'Gene'}) )
{
print "Key exists\n";
}
else
{
print "Key does not exists\n";
}
```

Output:
Key exists

> **Explanation:** The exists function returns true if the key is present in the hash, irrespective of the value is defined or not, and false otherwise.

Boolean operators

There are cases in which more than one conditions require to be true. Such cases can be checked with the help of nested if (if inside if).

if (expression)
{

Code block of first if;
    if (expression)
    {
    Code block of second if;   **Second if**   **First if**
    }

}

In this program if the first expression evaluates to be true only then it comes inside the code block of first if where it finds another if and evaluates it. If the code block of second if evaluates to be true then it executes the code block of second if.

Program 6.19
```perl
# Program to check whether a key exists in associative arrays using nested if
use strict;
use warnings;

my %Gene_length = ( 'MDR' => 2400, 'BRAC' => 2100, 'Rubisco' => 1800);
my %Protein_length = ( 'MDR' => 800, 'BRAC' => 700, 'Rubisco' => 600);

if (exists ($Gene_length{'MDR'}) )
{
        if (exists ($Protein_length{'MDR'}) )
        {
        print "Key exist in both associative arrays\n";
```

```
            }
    }
```

Output:
Key exist in both associative arrays

Explanation: Since the expression of first if is true only then it comes inside the code block of first if where it finds another if that also evaluates true therefore executes the code block of second if which contains print statement.

Notice the indentation of second if. It is used to write much clearer and readable programs. It is also a good practice to keep opening and closing curly braces in vertical line. While testing for existence of key in more than one associative array, two if statements has been used in the above program. The method works successfully. However Perl provides cleaner and easier way to do the same with Boolean operators. These operators evaluate multiple expressions and combine their results.

Boolean operators	Description
&&	AND operator works if expression on both sides evaluates true
||	OR operator works if expression on either side evaluates true
!	NOT operator is an unary operator which returns the logical negation of the expression (converts true condition to false and false condition to true)

Program 6.20
```
# Program to check whether a key exists in associative arrays using AND
# operator
use strict;
use warnings;

my %Gene_length = ( 'MDR' => 2400, 'BRAC' => 2100, 'Rubisco' => 1800);
```

79

```
my %Protein_length = ( 'MDR' => 800, 'BRAC' => 700, 'Rubisco' => 600);

if (exists ($Gene_length{'MDR'}) && exists ($Protein_length{'MDR'}) )
{
print "Key exist in both associative arrays\n";
}
```

Output:
Key exist in both associative arrays

Explanation: If checks the first expression and evaluates it true then it checks the second expression that is also true. Since expressions on both side of AND operator are true therefore it executes the print statement.

More than two expressions can also be clubbed in AND operator. In that case all expressions must be true to make the combined result of evaluation true.

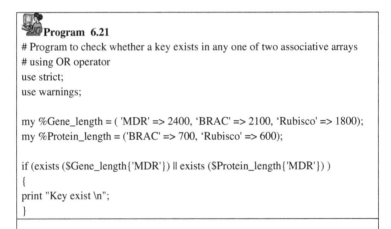

Program 6.21
```
# Program to check whether a key exists in any one of two associative arrays
# using OR operator
use strict;
use warnings;

my %Gene_length = ( 'MDR' => 2400, 'BRAC' => 2100, 'Rubisco' => 1800);
my %Protein_length = ('BRAC' => 700, 'Rubisco' => 600);

if (exists ($Gene_length{'MDR'}) || exists ($Protein_length{'MDR'}) )
{
print "Key exist \n";
}
```

Output:
Key exist

Explanation: If checks the first expression and evaluates it true consequently the code block executes. Since any of the expression requires to be true in OR operator therefore it does not check for second expression. In case the first expression in OR operator fails only then it checks the second expression.

Program 6.22

```perl
# Program to use NOT operator
use strict;
use warnings;

my %Gene_length = ('MDR' => 2400, 'BRAC' => 2100, 'Rubisco' => 1800,
'Gene');

if (! defined ($Gene_length{'Gene'}) )
{
print "Key contains a undefined value\n";
}
```

Output:
Key contains a undefined value

Explanation: The expression itself says "if not (!) defined the value of Gene key in %Gene_length". The defined function returns a false and the NOT operator converts it to true therefore if code block executes.

Points to remember

- Comparison operators help to make choices.
- If is used to make choices. It executes the code block based on true evaluation of expression.
- Else provides a default alternative to if.
- Boolean operators AND and OR help to club multiple expressions in single statement.

Test Yourself

1. Write a program to check the equality of numbers.
2. Write a program to calculate the percentage of a student and print the division.
3. Write a program to check non-equality of strings.
4. Write a program to use nested if.

Find errors

Program E6.1

```
use strict;
use warnings;

my $a = 8;
my $b = 4;

if ($a == $b)
{
print "The value stored in \$a is less than \$b\n";
else
{
print "The value stored in \$a is greater than \$b\n";
}
```

Output:
Error message

Program E6.2

```
use strict;
use warnings;

my $a = 3;
my $b = 4;

if ($a < $b)
{
print "The value stored in \$a is less than \$b\n";
}

elseif ($a > $b)
{
print "The value stored in \$a is greater than \$b\n";
}
```

```
else
{
print "The value stored in \$a is equal to \$b\n";
}
```

Output:
Error message

Chapter 7

Loops

Loops help to repeat the statements without rewriting them. Loop executes same statements again and again until a stop condition is reached. In loops there is an entry condition and exit condition both of which are very important in starting and ending a loop. If a loop is started without a proper exit condition it becomes an infinite loop. Beginners usually do such mistakes by creating an infinite loop. Loops are classified as determinate and indeterminate. For, while and foreach loops are some commonly used loops in Perl.

For loop

For is a determinate loop which carry an exit condition from beginning.

for (initialization; condition; modification)

{

Code block;

}

Program 7.1
```
# Program to print a series of numbers from 0-9 using for loop
use strict;
use warnings;

for (my $i = 0; $i <= 9; $i++)
{
print "i = $i\n";
}
```

Output:
i = 0
i = 1
i = 2
i = 3
i = 4
i = 5
i = 6
i = 7
i = 8
i = 9

Explanation: In the loop, first the value of scalar variable $i is initialized to 0. Then it checks whether the value of $i is less than or equal to 9. Since 0 is less than 9 therefore the condition evaluates true and it comes in the code block and prints the statement i = 0. The execution now transfers to the modification where it autoincrement the value of $i to 1 (0 + 1 = 1). It again checks the condition whether the value of $i is less than or equal to 9. Since 1 is less than 9 therefore the condition evaluates true and it comes in the code block and prints the statement i = 1. It continues in the same fashion until it reaches the condition when the value of $i = 10. At this stage the condition evaluates to be false (10 <= 9) and the loop exits without further iteration.

While loop

While is an indeterminate loop which rely on code block to modify the exit condition to exit the loop.

Initialization;
While (condition)
{
Code block;
Modification;
}

Program 7.2

```
# Program to print a series of numbers from 0-9 using while loop
use strict;
use warnings;

my $i = 0;
while ($i <= 9)
{
print "i = $i\n";
$i++;
}
```

Output:
```
i = 0
i = 1
i = 2
i = 3
i = 4
i = 5
i = 6
i = 7
i = 8
i = 9
```

Foreach loop

Foreach loop is specifically designed to iterate over all indexes of array starting from 0th index. There is no need to initialize the value, test the condition and modification in foreach loop.

Program 7.3

```
# Program to print elements of array using foreach loop
use strict;
use warnings;

my @array = qw (gene1 gene2 gene3 gene4 gene5 gene6) ;

foreach my $element (@array)
{
```

```
print "$element\n";
}
```

Output:

gene1

gene2

gene3

gene4

gene5

gene6

Explanation: Foreach loop automatically starts from the 0th index of array and exit itself when reaches to last index of array. The advantage of using loops in printing array elements is that there is no need to specify all indexes specifically, which can be a tedious process for large arrays. A loop can iterate over all indexes, one by one, of an array in an automatic fashion.

One loop can be used in place of another to do most of the task. For example, array elements can also be accessed using for and while loop. However one loop cannot be replaced with another in all cases.

Program 7.4

```
# Program to print elements of array using for loop
use strict;
use warnings;

my @array = qw (gene1 gene2 gene3 gene4 gene5 gene6);

for (my $i = 0; $i <= $#array; $i++)
{
print "The array element stored in $i index is: $array[$i] \n";
}
```

Output:
The array element stored in 0 index is: gene1
The array element stored in 1 index is: gene2
The array element stored in 2 index is: gene3
The array element stored in 3 index is: gene4
The array element stored in 4 index is: gene5
The array element stored in 5 index is: gene6

Program 7.5

```perl
# Program to print elements of array using while loop
use strict;
use warnings;

my @array = qw (gene1 gene2 gene3 gene4 gene5 gene6);

my $i = 0;
while ($i <= $#array)
{
print "Index $i stores: $array[$i]\n";
$i++;
}
```

Output:
Index 0 stores: gene1
Index 1 stores: gene2
Index 2 stores: gene3
Index 3 stores: gene4
Index 4 stores: gene5
Index 5 stores: gene6

Program 7.6

```perl
# Program to print each key-value pair of associative array
# in new line using foreach
use strict;
use warnings;
```

```
my %Gene_length = ( 'MDR' => 2400,'BRAC' => 2267,'Rubisco' => 1700) ;
print %Gene_length,"\n";

my @key = keys (%Gene_length) ;

foreach my $key (@key)
{
print "The value associated with key $key is: $Gene_length{$key} ","\n";
}
```

Output:
MDR2400Rubisco1700BRAC2267
The value associated with key MDR is: 2400
The value associated with key Rubisco is: 1700
The value associated with key BRAC is: 2267

Program 7.7

```
# Program to print each key-value pair of associative array
# in new line using while loop
use strict;
use warnings;

my %Gene_length = ( 'MDR' => 2400,'BRAC' => 2267,'Rubisco' => 1700) ;

my @key = keys (%Gene_length);

my $i = 0;
while ($i <= $#key)
{
print "The value associated with $key[$i] is: $Gene_length{$key[$i]} ","\n";
$i++;
}
```

Output:
The value associated with Rubisco is: 1700
The value associated with BRAC is: 2267
The value associated with MDR is: 2400

Program 7.8

```
# Program to print values of associative array in new line using for loop
use strict;
use warnings;

my %Gene_length = ( 'MDR' => 2400,'BRAC' => 2267,'Rubisco' => 1700) ;

my @value = values (%Gene_length) ;

print "The values are:\n";
for (my $i = 0; $i <= $#value; $i++)
{
print "$value[$i] \n";
}
```

Output:
The values are:
2400
2267
1700

Program 7.9

```
# Program to print key-value pair of associative array using each function
use strict;
use warnings;

my %Gene_length = ( 'MDR' => 2400,'BRAC' => 2267,'Rubisco' => 1700);

print "The key-value pairs in \%Gene_length are:\n";
while ( ( (my $key, my $value) = each (%Gene_length) )
{
print "$key => $value\n";
}
```

Output:
The key-value pairs in %Gene_length are:

```
BRAC => 2267
Rubisco => 1700
MDR => 2400
```

Loop exits

Last terminates the loop without executing further iterations of loop when a desired condition evaluates true. Next skips the current iteration and starts the next iteration of loop.

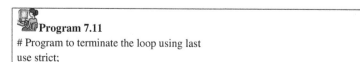**Program 7.10**
```
# Program to skip iteration of loop using next
use strict;
use warnings;

for (my $i = 0; $i <= 5; $i++)
{
        if ($i == 4) {
        next;
        }
print "i = $i\n";
}
```

Output:
```
i = 0
i = 1
i = 2
i = 3
i = 5
```

Explanation: When if condition evaluates true the loop iteration skips execution of print statement and starts next iteration. As a result the value i = 4 does not appears in the output.

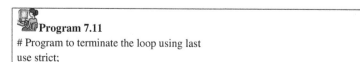**Program 7.11**
```
# Program to terminate the loop using last
use strict;
```

```
use warnings;

for (my $i = 0; $i <= 10; $i++)
{
        if ($i == 5)  {
        last;
        }
print "i = $i\n";
}
```

Output:
i = 0
i = 1
i = 2
i = 3
i = 4

Explanation: When if condition evaluates true the loop terminates. As a result the value of i from 1- 4 appears in the output.

Points to remember

- For loop is used when prior to execution number of iterations are known.
- Foreach is suitable to iterate over all indexes of an array.
- While is an indeterminate type of loop.

Test Yourself

1. Write a program to print a series of numbers from 10 to 1 using while loop.
2. Write a program to print series of even number upto 100 using for loop.
3. Write a program to print key-value pairs of an associative array in the following format:
   Key1 => Value1
   Key2 => Value2
4. Create an array of numbers and get the sum of all values stored in each index of array using foreach loop.

Find errors

Program E7.1
```perl
use strict;
use warnings;

for (my $i = 0; $i = 9; $i++)
{
print "i = $i\n";
}
```

Output:
```
i = 9
i = 9
i = 9
i = 9
i = 9
i = 9
i = 9
i = 9
i = 9
i = 9
i = 9
i = 9
.
.
.
i = 9
i = 9
i = 9
```

Program E7.2
```perl
use strict;
use warnings;
my $i = 1;
while($i <=10)
{
print "$i\n";
```

```
}
```

Output:
```
1
1
1
.
.
1
1
1
```

Chapter 8

Regular Expressions

Regular expressions also known as regex are the tools to perform pattern matching, substitution and translation. Regular expressions use binding operator, equal to sign followed by a tilde (=~), to create syntax for string manipulation. There are three regular expression operators frequently used in Perl:

Operator	Description
m	Match operator used to match a pattern in a string $string =~ m/ATG/;
s	Substitute operator replaces a complete pattern with another pattern $string =~ s/ATG/tac/; Here ATG is the pattern to be replaced with tac. Substitute operator first search for ATG pattern and then substitute it with tac. Therefore the entire pattern (ATG) will be replaced by another pattern (tac).
tr	Translate operator acts on individual characters of a pattern to replace characters at corresponding positions in another pattern $string =~ tr/ATG/tac/; Translate operator first looks for A in the string and replace it by t. It will replace T with a, and G with c. Therefore there is one to

one correspondance between characters of a pattern that has to be replaced with characters of another pattern. By default translate operator acts on entire length of string.

There are optional switches which works with regular expression operators.

Switch works with match operator:

Switch	Description
g	Global search
i	Insensitive to case
o	only evaluate once

Switch works with substitute operator:

Switch	Description
g	Global search
e	Evaluate
i	Insensitive to case
o	Only evaluate once

Switch works with translate operator:

Switch	Description
c	Complement (Do not confuse with biological complement)
d	Delete
s	Squeeze

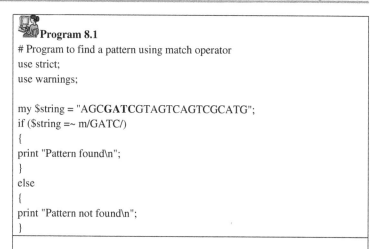

Program 8.1

```
# Program to find a pattern using match operator
use strict;
use warnings;

my $string = "AGCGATCGTAGTCAGTCGCATG";
if ($string =~ m/GATC/)
{
print "Pattern found\n";
}
else
{
print "Pattern not found\n";
}
```

Output:
Pattern found

Explanation: When used in scalar context the match operator either returns a true or a false value. Since pattern is found in this case therefore if code block executes.

The use of m in match operator is optional. If a pattern is provided in between // Perl understands that it has to match the pattern.

Program 8.2

```
# Program to find a pattern
use strict;
use warnings;

my $string = "AGCGATCGTAGTCAGTCGCATG";
if ($string =~ /GATC/)   # m is optional
{
print "Pattern found\n";
}
else
{
print "Pattern not found\n";
}
```

97

Output:
Pattern found

Program 8.3

```
# Program to find a pattern and count number of occurrences
use strict;
use warnings;

my $string = "AGCGATCGTAGATCAGTCGATCATG";
my @patterns = $string =~ m/GATC/g;
print "String has ", scalar(@patterns)," patterns\n";
```

Output:

String has 3 patterns

Explanation: When used in array context with global switch the match operator returns all patterns identified. The number of patterns returned can be easily counted by knowing the size of array.

Program 8.4

```
# Program to perform case sensitive search of a pattern
use strict;
use warnings;

my $string = "AGCGATCGTAGTCAGTCGCATG";
if ($string =~ m/gatc/)
{
print "Pattern found\n";
}
else
{
print "Pattern not found\n";
```

```
}
```

Output:

Pattern not found

Explanation: The string is in capital letters however the pattern is in small letters. Therefore despite of presence of pattern in string the match operator is unable to find the pattern.

Program 8.5

```perl
# Program to perform case insensitive search of a pattern
use strict;
use warnings;

my $string = "AGCGATCGTAGTCAGTCGCATG";
if ($string =~ m/gatc/i)
{
print "Pattern found\n";
}
else
{
print "Pattern not found\n";
}
```

Output:

Pattern found

Explanation: The search has been made case insensitive by using i switch therefore pattern found.

Program 8.6

```perl
# Program to substitute a pattern using substitute operator
use strict;
```

```
use warnings;

my $patt = "AGACTATGCTATG";
print "Pattern is: $patt\n";
$patt =~ s/ATG/atg/;
print "Substituted pattern is: $patt\n";
```

Output:
Pattern is: AGACT**ATG**CT**ATG**
Substituted pattern is: AGACT**atg**CT**ATG**

This program does not substitute all occurrences of ATG because global [g] switch is not used.

Program 8.7
```
# Program to substitute all occurrences of a pattern using substitute operator
use strict;
use warnings;

my $patt = "AGACTATGCTATG";
print "Pattern is: $patt\n";
$patt =~ s/ATG/atg/g;
print "Substituted pattern is: $patt\n";
```

Output:
Pattern is: AGACT**ATG**CT**ATG**
Substituted pattern is: AGACT**atg**CT**atg**

Program 8.8
```
# Program to substitute pattern in case insensitive mode
use strict;
use warnings;

my $patt = "AGACTATGCTATG";
print "Pattern is: $patt\n";
$patt =~ s/atg/atg/g;
print "No substitution occurs: $patt\n";
```

```
$patt =~ s/atg/atg/ig;
print "Substituted pattern is: $patt\n";
```

Output:
Pattern is: AGACT**ATG**CT**ATG**
No substitution occurs: AGACT**ATG**CT**ATG**
Substituted pattern is: AGACT**atg**CT**atg**

Explanation: The first attempt has been made to substitute atg with atg. However atg is not present in $patt instead ATG is present. Therefore no substitution occurs. When the switch **i** is used with substitute operator then it substitutes the pattern.

Program 8.9
```
# Program to generate complementary sequence using tr operator
use strict;
use warnings;

my $string = "AGCGATCGTAGTCAGTCGCATG";
print "$string\t#Sequence \n";

$string =~ tr/AGCT/TCGA/;
print "$string\t#Complimentary sequence \n";
```

Output:
AGCGATCGTAGTCAGTCGCATG #Sequence
TCGCTAGCATCAGTCAGCGTAC #Complimentary sequence

Explanation: Translate operator does not look for AGCT pattern to translate into TCGA. Instead it finds A and translate it into T. Similarly G → C, C → G and T → A have been translated. There is no need for global switch here since tr operates globally on a string.

Program 8.10

```
# Program to replace ambiguous characters from DNA sequence
use strict;
use warnings;

my $sequence = "GCGTANXXCGTTXNATAATCGGTANNGTC";
print "Sequence is: $sequence\n";
$sequence =~ tr/ATGC/ /c; #complement (Other than ATGC)
print "Modified sequence is: $sequence\n";
```

Output:

Sequence is: GCGTA**NXX**CGTT**X**NATAATCGGTA**NN**GTC

Modified sequence is: GCGTA   CGTT ATAATCGGTA GTC

Explanation: The complement switch used with the translate operator looks for characters other than ATGC and replace them with a space. These spaces appear in the output. Characters other than ATGC can also be provided in the pattern in that case switch [c] does not look for characters provided in the pattern.

The tr operator can be used to count sequence characters.

Program 8.11

```
# Program to count characters in a sequence
use strict;
use warnings;

my $sequence = "AGCGATCGTAGTCAGTCGCATG";
print "$sequence\t#Sequence before count \n";
my $count = $sequence =~ tr/ATGC//;
print "$sequence\t#Sequence after count \n";
print "No. of sequence characters: $count\n";
```

Output:

AGCGATCGTAGTCAGTCGCATG #Sequence before count

AGCGATCGTAGTCAGTCGCATG #Sequence after count
No. of sequence characters: 22

Explanation: Translate operator returns a scalar value showing the number of replacements made. The sequence remains unchanged after counting. The tr operator treats the pattern and the pattern to be replaced as same if no space is provided in between //. Remember not to provide the space between //, otherwise tr will replace all ATGC to space.

Program 8.12

```
# Program to count characters in a sequence and replace them
use strict;
use warnings;

my $sequence = "AGCGATCGTAGTCAGTCGCATG";
print "$sequence\t#Sequence before count \n";
my $count = $sequence =~ tr/ATGC/ /;   #/ / with space
print "$sequence\t#Sequence after count \n";
print "No. of replaced characters: $count\n";
```

Output:

AGCGATCGTAGTCAGTCGCATG #Sequence before count
                        #Sequence after count
No. of replaced characters: 22

Explanation: Since space is provided in between / / therefore tr operator replaced all ATGC to space and no character remains in the sequence.

Program 8.13

```
# Program to replace ambiguous characters from DNA
```

```
# sequence and count them
use strict;
use warnings;

my $sequence = "GCGTANXXCGTTXNATAATCGGTANNGTC";
print "$sequence\t#Sequence\n";
my $countN = $sequence =~ tr/ATGC/ /c;
print "$sequence\t#Modified sequence\n";
print "No. of N and X replaced are: $countN\n";
```

Output:

GCGTANXXCGTTXNATAATCGGTANNGTC #Sequence

GCGTA   CGTT   ATAATCGGTA   GTC #Modified sequence

No. of N and X replaced are: 7

Program 8.14

```
# Program to replace ambiguous characters from DNA
# sequence and squeeze the gaps
use strict;
use warnings;

my $sequence = "GCGTANXXCGTTXNATAATCGGTANNGTC";
print "$sequence\t#Sequence\n";
$sequence =~ tr/ATGC/ /cs;    #squeeze
print "$sequence\t#Modified and squeeze sequence \n";
```

Output:

GCGTANXXCGTTXNATAATCGGTANNGTC #Sequence

GCGTA CGTT ATAATCGGTA GTC   # Squeezed gaps

Explanation: The multiple gaps have been squeezed to single gaps by using squeeze [s] switch.

Program 8.15

```perl
# Program to replace ambiguous characters from DNA
# sequence and delete the gaps
use strict;
use warnings;

my $sequence = "GCGTANXXCGTTXNATAATCGGTANNGTC";
print "$sequence\t#Sequence\n";
$sequence =~ tr/ATGC/ /cd;   #delete
print "$sequence\t#Deleted gaps\n";
```

Output:

GCGTANXXCGTTXNATAATCGGTANNGTC   #Sequence

GCGTACGTTATAATCGGTAGTC #Deleted gaps

Program 8.16

```perl
# Program to find patterns like GAA, GTA, GCA, GGA
use strict;
use warnings;

my @patt;
my                              $sequence                    =
"GCTGACGTACGTATGCAGTCTATAATCGTACGTAGGCATGGAT";
if (@patt = $sequence =~ m/G.A/g)
{
print "Pattern found\n";
}
else
{
print "Pattern not found\n";
}
print "@patt\n";
```

Output:
Pattern found
GTA GTA GCA GTA GTA GCA GGA

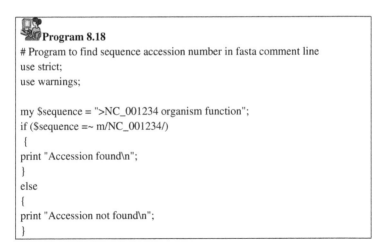

Program 8.17

```
# Program to find patterns with specific choices
use strict;
use warnings;

my @patt;
my                              $sequence                        =
"GCTGACGTACGTATGCAGTCTATAATCGTACGTAGGCATGGAT";
if (@patt = $sequence =~ m/G[ATGC]A/g)
{
print "Pattern found\n";
}
else
{
print "Pattern not found\n";
}
print "@patt\n";
```

Output:
Pattern found
GTA GTA GCA GTA GTA GCA GGA

Program 8.18

```
# Program to find sequence accession number in fasta comment line
use strict;
use warnings;

my $sequence = ">NC_001234 organism function";
if ($sequence =~ m/NC_001234/)
{
print "Accession found\n";
}
else
{
print "Accession not found\n";
}
```

Output:
Accession found

Program 8.19
```perl
# Program to find sequence accession number using quantifiers
use strict;
use warnings;

my $sequence = ">NC_001234 organism function";
if ($sequence =~ m/[A-Z]*_[0-9]*/)  # range
{
print "Accession found\n";
}
else
{
print "Accession not found\n";
}
```

Output:
Accession found

Program 8.20
```perl
# Program to use backslash escaped characters
# to find sequence accession number
use strict;
use warnings;

my $sequence = ">NC_001234 organism function";
if ($sequence =~ m/\w*_\d*/)
{
print "Accession found\n";
}
else
{
print "Accession not found\n";
```

}

Output:
Accession found

Program 8.21
```
# Program to find a pattern using quantifier symbol ?
use strict;
use warnings;

my $sequence = "ATGCGT";
if ($sequence =~ m/(CGT)?/g)
{
print "Pattern found\n";
}
else
{
print "Pattern not found\n";
}
```

Output:
Pattern found

Program 8.22
```
# Program to find a pattern 0 or 1 times
use strict;
use warnings;

my $sequence = "ATG";
if ($sequence =~ m/(CGT){0,1}/g)
{
print "Pattern found\n";
}
else
```

```
{
print "Pattern not found\n";
}
```

Output:
Pattern found

Explanation: By quantifying minimum and maximum number of occurrences of a pattern, a range can be provided to search for pattern.

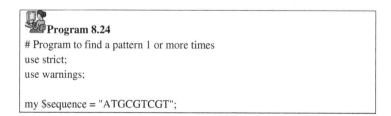**Program 8.23**

```
# Program to find a pattern using quantifier symbol +
use strict;
use warnings;

my $sequence = "ATG";
if ($sequence =~ m/(CGT)+/g)
{
print "Pattern found\n";
}
else
{
print "Pattern not found\n";
}
```

Output:
Pattern not found

Program 8.24

```
# Program to find a pattern 1 or more times
use strict;
use warnings;

my $sequence = "ATGCGTCGT";
```

```
if ($sequence =~ m/(CGT){1,}/g)
{
print "Pattern found\n";
}
else
{
print "Pattern not found\n";
}
```

Output:

Pattern found

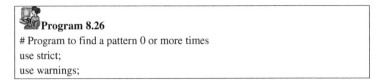

Program 8.25

```
# Program to find a pattern using quantifier symbol *
use strict;
use warnings;

my $sequence = "ATG";
if ($sequence =~ m/(CGT)*/g)
{
print "Pattern found\n";
}
else
{
print "Pattern not found\n";
}
```

Output:

Pattern found

Program 8.26

```
# Program to find a pattern 0 or more times
use strict;
use warnings;
```

```
my $sequence = "ATGCGTCGTCGTATGCGTAGCT";
if ($sequence =~ m/(CGT){0,}/g)
{
print "Pattern found\n";
}
else
{
print "Pattern not found\n";
}
```

Output:
Pattern found

Program 8.27
```
# Program to find a pattern exactly 3 times
use strict;
use warnings;

my                          $sequence                          =
"GCTGACGTACGTATGCAGTCTATAATCGTACGTAGTCATGCGT";

if ($sequence =~ m/(CGT){3}/g)  #CGTCGTCGT
{
print "Pattern found\n";
}
else
{
print "Pattern not found\n";
}
```

Output:
Pattern not found

Program 8.28
Program to find a pattern exactly 3 or more times
use strict;
use warnings;

my $sequence   =
"GCTGACGTACGTATGCAGTCTATAATCGTACGTAGTCATGCGT";

if ($sequence =~ m/(CGT){3,}/g)
{
print "Pattern found\n";
}
else
{
print "Pattern not found\n";
}

Output:
Pattern not found

Program 8.29
Program to find a pattern with minimum 3 and maximum 5 occurrences
use strict;
use warnings;

my $sequence   =
"GCTTGACGTTTACGTATGCGTAGTCTATTTTAATTTTTTCGTA";
my @patt;
if (@patt = $sequence =~ m/T{3,5}/g)
{
print "Pattern found\n";
}
else
{
print "Pattern not found\n";
}
print "@patt\n";

> **Output:**
> Pattern found
> TTT TTTT TTTTT

Points to remember

- Match operator [m] is used to match a pattern.
- Substitute operator [s] substitute one pattern with another pattern.
- There is one to one correspondence between characters when translate operator [tr] is used.

Test Yourself

1. Write a program to remove ambiguous characters from DNA sequence.
2. Write a program to count number of amino acid residues in a protein sequence.
3. Write a program to replace all occurrences of ATG with atg in a DNA sequence.
4. Write a program to find a pattern and count all occurrences.

Find errors

> **Program E8.1**
> ```
> use strict;
> use warnings;
>
> my $string = "AGCGATCGTAGTCAGTCGCATG";
> if ($string = m/GATC/)
> {
> print "Pattern found\n";
> }
> else
> {
> print "Pattern not found\n";
> }
> ```

Output:
Pattern not found

Program E8.2
use strict;
use warnings;

my $patt = "AGACTATGCTATG";
print "Pattern is: $patt\n";
$patt =~ /ATG/atg/g;
print "Substituted pattern is: $patt\n";

Output:
Error message

Chapter 9

Functions for Strings

There are functions to know the length of a string, to reverse a string, split a string, to know the position of a substring etc.

Function	Description
Length	The length function calculates the length of a string.
Reverse	Reverse function reverses a string.
Split	Split function breaks a string.
Index	The index function takes a string and finds the substring starting from the position specified.

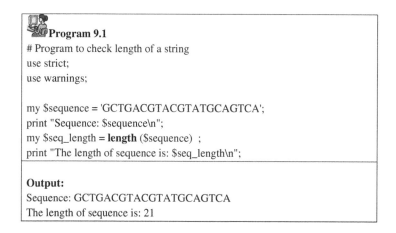

Program 9.1
```
# Program to check length of a string
use strict;
use warnings;

my $sequence = 'GCTGACGTACGTATGCAGTCA';
print "Sequence: $sequence\n";
my $seq_length = length ($sequence) ;
print "The length of sequence is: $seq_length\n";
```

Output:
Sequence: GCTGACGTACGTATGCAGTCA
The length of sequence is: 21

Program 9.2
Program to reverse a string
use strict;
use warnings;

my $sequence = 'GCTGACGTACGTATGCAGTCA';
print "$sequence \t #Sequence \n";
my $rev_seq = **reverse** ($sequence) ;
print "$rev_seq \t #Reversed sequence \n";

Output:
GCTGACGTACGTATGCAGTCA   #Sequence
ACTGACGTATGCATGCAGTCG   #Reverse sequence

Program 9.3
Program to break a string from desired character
use strict;
use warnings;

my $sequence = 'GCTGACGTACGTATGCAGTCA';
print "Sequence: $sequence\n";
my @seq_split = split/**T**/, $sequence;
print "After Split: @seq_split\n";

Output:
Sequence: GCTGACGTACGTATGCAGTCA
After Split: GC GACG ACG A GCAG CA

Explanation: The split function breaks the string from the pattern provided. Since T is given as a pattern to split from, therefore split breaks the sequence wherever it finds T. Since there are several T present in the sequence, therefore, an array is a suitable variable to hold remaining sequence characters. The characters before first T will store in 0th index of array. The characters after first T will store in 1st index of array and so on.

Program 9.4
Program to break a string from individual characters
use strict;
use warnings;

my $sequence = 'GCTGACGTACGTATGCAGTCATGG';
print "Sequence: $sequence\n";
my @seq_split = split//, $sequence;
print "After Split: @seq_split\n";

Output:
Sequence: GCTGACGTACGTATGCAGTCATGG
After Split: G C T G A C G T A C G T A T G C A G T C A T G G

Explanation: The split function breaks the string from individual characters if no space is provided between //. Each character assigned to individual array index in the same order. The first character G will store in 0th index, second character C will store in 1st index of array and so on.

Index function treats string as an array, which is actually not an array, by considering the position of string characters starting form 0.

Index	0	1	2	3	4	5
String Characters	A	T	T	G	C	A

index(String, Substring, Position);

Program 9.5
Program to find the index of a substring
use strict;
use warnings;

my $sequence = 'ACGTACGTATGCAGTACGTGGCTGA';
print "Sequence: $sequence\n";

```
my $position = index ($sequence,'TACGT',0)  ;
print "The position of TACGT is: $position \n";
```

Output:
Sequence: ACGTACGTATGCAGTACGTGGCTGA
The position of TACGT is: 3

Explanation: The index function looks for substring TACGT in the string $sequence starting from position 0 and it finds it at position 3. Since index treats string as an array therefore the position of first character is 0 and so on. The starting position of substring TACGT is 4 (Since humans are familiar to start counting from 1) however due to array like treatment of string by index function it shows the position of substring TACGT as 3. Notice that index function only finds the first substring in the string. However substring is present one more time in the same string.

To find all positions of substring, the index function has to be used with while loop.

Program 9.6
```
# Program to find all positions of a substring
use strict;
use warnings;

my $sequence = 'ACGTACGTATGCAGTACGTGGCTGA';
print "Sequence: $sequence\n";

my $posi = 0;
my @substring_posi = ();

while ( ($posi = index ($sequence,'TACGT',$posi)) >= 0)
{
push(@substring_posi, $posi);
$posi++;
}

print "All positions of TACGT: ", join(',',@substring_posi)," \n";
```

Output:
Sequence: ACGTACGTATGCAGTACGTGGCTGA
All positions of TACGT: 3,14

Explanation: To find all positions of a substring the while loop evaluates to be true if position find downstream of $posi. In case substring does not found then index function returns a -1 and while evaluates false. If substring found the position is stored in an array. The position is autoincremented to search for more substring further from that position.

Substr function retrieve a substring from a string provided the start position and length to be retrieved. This function also treats a string as an array.

substr(String, Start, Length);

Program 9.7
\# Program to retrieve a substring from a string
use strict;
use warnings;

my $string = 'ACGTACGTATGCAGTACGTGGCTGA';
print "Sequence: $string\n";
my $sub_string = substr ($string,1,10) ;
print "The substring retrieved is: $sub_string \n";

Output:
Sequence: A**CGTACGTAT**GCAGTACGTGGCTGA
The substring retrieved is: CGTACGTATG

Explanation: Since substr function starts indexing of a string from 0, therefore it retrieves the substring starting from character C with 1 position upto 10 length.

Points to remember
- Length function calculates the length of a string.

- Reverse function reverses a string.
- Split function breaks a string from desired characters.
- The index function tells the position of a substring in a string.
- The substr function retrieves the desired substring from a string.

Test Yourself

1. Write a program to calculate the length of a string.
2. Write a program to retrieve a substring and reverse it.
3. Write a program to break the string into individual characters.
4. Write a program to know the position of a substring in a string.

Find errors

Program E9.1

```
use strict;
use warnings;

my $sequence = 'GCTGACGTACGTATGCAGTCA';
print "Sequence: $sequence\n";
my @seq_split = split/T/ $sequence;
print "After Split: @seq_split\n";
```

Output:
Error message

Program E9.2

```
use strict;
use warnings;

my $string = 'ACGTACGTATGCAGTACGTGGCTGA';
print "Sequence: $string\n";
my $sub_string = substr (string,2,10)  ;
print "The substring retrieved is: $sub_string \n";
```

Output:
Error message

Chapter 10

References

A reference is a scalar that refers to a variable. The variable can be a scalar, array or associative array. To create a reference the reference operator, '\', is prefixed with variable name. References help to pass arrays and associative arrays to subroutine. Moreover complex data structures including array of arrays can be created using references.

Program 10.1

```
# Program to create reference to scalar variable
use strict;
use warnings;

my $scalar = 4;
print "Scalar Value: $scalar\n";
my $scalar_ref = \$scalar;
print "Reference: $scalar_ref\n";
```

Output:
Scalar Value: 4
Reference: SCALAR(0x44444c)

Since the memory is allocated during the execution of a program, therefore, the value for a reference in your output differs from the value shown above.

The reference has to be dereferenced to get the value of referent (the variable whose reference is created). To dereference a reference, prefix the sign used to define a variable ($, @ or %) with reference.

Program 10.2

```perl
# Program to dereference a reference
use strict;
use warnings;

my $scalar = 4;
print "Scalar Value: $scalar\n";
my $scalar_ref = \$scalar;
print "Reference: $scalar_ref\n";
print "Dereference: $$scalar_ref\n";
print "Dereference: ${$scalar_ref}\n"; # both statements correct
```

Output:
Scalar Value: 4
Reference: SCALAR(0x1eb444c)
Dereference: 4
Dereference: 4

Explanation: As a reference of scalar variable has been created therefore to dereference it a $ sign is prefixed with reference.

Similarly the reference of array and associative array can be created.

Program 10.3

```perl
# Program to create reference to array and dereference it
use strict;
use warnings;

my @array = qw(4 69 ATGC);
print "Array: @array\n";
my $array_ref = \@array;
print "Reference: $array_ref\n";
print "Dereference: @{$array_ref}\n";
```

Output:

Array: 4 69 ATGC
Reference: ARRAY(0x1d2444c)
Dereference: 4 69 ATGC

> **Explanation:** As a reference of array variable has been created therefore to dereference it a @ sign is prefixed with reference.

The value stored in specific index of an array can directly be accessed using reference to that array.

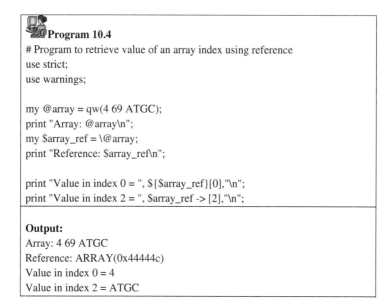

Program 10.4
```
# Program to retrieve value of an array index using reference
use strict;
use warnings;

my @array = qw(4 69 ATGC);
print "Array: @array\n";
my $array_ref = \@array;
print "Reference: $array_ref\n";

print "Value in index 0 = ", ${$array_ref}[0],"\n";
print "Value in index 2 = ", $array_ref -> [2],"\n";
```

Output:
```
Array: 4 69 ATGC
Reference: ARRAY(0x44444c)
Value in index 0 = 4
Value in index 2 = ATGC
```

The reference to an array or associative array can be created directly without their separate declaration. Such referents are called anonymous referents because they do not have any name.

Program 10.5
```
# Program to create anonymous array
use strict;
use warnings;

my $array_ref = [4, 69, 'ATGC'];
print "Reference: $array_ref\n";
```

```
print "Dereference: @{$array_ref}\n";
```

Output:
Reference: ARRAY(0x727b94)
Dereference: 4 69 ATGC

Explanation: To create anonymous array [ ] are used instead of ( ). It will directly create a reference to array which can be stored in scalar variable.

Program 10.6
```
# Program to create reference to associative array and dereference it
use strict;
use warnings;

my %associative_array = ( 'MDR', 2400,'BRAC', 2267,'Rubisco', 1700) ;
print "Key-value pairs in associative array: ",%associative_array ,"\n";
my $associative_array_ref = \%associative_array ;
print "Reference: $associative_array_ref\n";
print "Dereference: ", %{$associative_array_ref},"\n";
```

Output:
Key-value pairs in associative array: MDR2400Rubisco1700BRAC2267
Reference: HASH(0x57444c)
Dereference: MDR2400Rubisco1700BRAC2267

Explanation: As a reference of associative array has been created therefore to dereference it a % sign is prefixed with reference.

The value associated with a key of an associative array can directly be accessed using reference to that associative array.

Program 10.7

```perl
# Program to retrieve value associated with a key using reference
use strict;
use warnings;

my %associative_array = ( 'MDR', 2400,'BRAC', 2267,'Rubisco', 1700) ;
print "Key-value pairs in associative array: ",%associative_array ,"\n";
my $associative_array_ref = \%associative_array ;
print "Reference: $associative_array_ref\n";

print    "Value    associated    with    key    MDR    is    =    ",
${$associative_array_ref}{'MDR'},"\n";
print "Value associated with key BRAC is = ", $associative_array_ref ->
{'BRAC'},"\n";
```

Output:
Key-value pairs in associative array: Rubisco1700BRAC2267MDR2400
Reference: HASH(0x1e0444c)
Value associated with key MDR is = 2400
Value associated with key BRAC is = 2267

Program 10.8

```perl
# Program to create anonymous associative array
use strict;
use warnings;

my $associative_array_ref = {'MDR', 2400,'BRAC', 2267,'Rubisco', 1700} ;
print "Reference: $associative_array_ref\n";
print "Dereference: ", %{$associative_array_ref},"\n";
```

Output:
Reference: HASH(0x3c7b94)
Dereference: BRAC2267MDR2400Rubisco1700

Explanation: To create anonymous associative array { } are used instead of ( ). The reference of which can be stored in scalar variable.

Program 10.9

```perl
# Program to create a reference of reference
use strict;
use warnings;

my $scalar = 4;
print "Scalar Value: $scalar\n";
my $scalar_ref = \$scalar;
print "Reference1: $scalar_ref\n";

my $scalar_ref1 = \$scalar_ref;
print "Reference2: $scalar_ref1\n";

my $scalar_ref2 = \$scalar_ref1;
print "Reference3: $scalar_ref2\n";

print "Dereference \$scalar_ref: ${$scalar_ref}\n";
print "Dereference \$scalar_ref1: ", $$$scalar_ref1,"\n";
print "Dereference \$scalar_ref2: ", $$$$scalar_ref2,"\n";
```

Output:
```
Scalar Value: 4
Reference1: SCALAR(0x1ea444c)
Reference2: REF(0x1ea4524)
Reference3: REF(0x1ec7bf4)
Dereference $scalar_ref: 4
Dereference $scalar_ref1: 4
Dereference $scalar_ref2: 4
```

Program 10.10

```perl
# Program to check type of referent
use strict;
use warnings;

my $scalar = 4;
print "Scalar Value: $scalar\n";
my $scalar_ref = \$scalar;
print "Scalar reference: $scalar_ref\n";
print "Type of referent: ",ref($scalar_ref),"\n";
print "Dereference \$scalar_ref: ${$scalar_ref}\n";
```

```
print "\n\n";

my $scalar_ref1 = \$scalar_ref;
print "Reference of scalar reference: $scalar_ref1\n";
print "Type of referent: ",ref($scalar_ref1),"\n";
print "Dereference \$scalar_ref1: ", $$$scalar_ref1,"\n";

print "\n\n";

my @array = qw(4 69 ATGC);
print "Array: @array\n";
my $array_ref = \@array;
print "Array reference: $array_ref\n";
print "Type of referent: ",ref($array_ref),"\n";
print "Dereference \$array_ref: @{$array_ref}\n";

print "\n\n";

my %associative_array = ( 'MDR', 2400,'BRAC', 2267,'Rubisco', 1700)  ;
print "Key-value pairs in associative array: ",%associative_array ,"\n";;
my $associative_array_ref = \%associative_array ;
print "Associative array reference: $associative_array_ref\n";
print "Type of referent: ",ref($associative_array_ref),"\n";
print "Dereference \$associative_array_ref: ", %{$associative_array_ref},"\n";
```

Output:
Scalar Value: 4
Scalar reference: SCALAR(0x1dc444c)
Type of referent: SCALAR
Dereference $scalar_ref: 4

Reference of scalar reference: REF(0x1dc4524)
Type of referent: REF
Dereference $scalar_ref1: 4

Array: 4 69 ATGC
Array reference: ARRAY(0x1dd7d34)
Type of referent: ARRAY
Dereference $array_ref: 4 69 ATGC

Key-value pairs in associative array: BRAC2267MDR2400Rubisco1700
Associative array reference: HASH(0x1dd7a64)

Type of referent: HASH
Dereference $associative_array_ref: BRAC2267MDR2400Rubisco1700

Explanation: The function ref returns the type of referent along with memory location.

Two dimensional arrays (Array of arrays)

The array of arrays stores individual arrays in each index. It is helpful in creating multidimensional data structures.

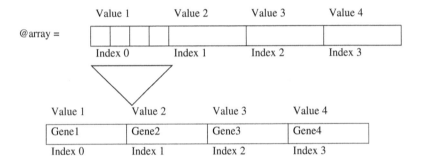

```
Program 10.11
# Program to create two dimensional array
use strict;
use warnings;

my $two_dimen_array = [ [1, 2, 3], [4, 5, 6], [7, 8, 9] ];

print "Reference: $two_dimen_array\n";
print "Dereference \$two_dimen_array:\n";
print "@{$two_dimen_array}\n";
print "\n";
print "Dereference    anonymous    array    stored    at    0th    index:    ",
"@{$two_dimen_array -> [0]}","\n";
```

```
print "Dereference and get the value stored at 0th index : ", $two_dimen_array
-> [0][0],"\n";
print "Dereference and get the value stored at 1st index : ", $two_dimen_array
-> [0]->[1],"\n";
print "\n";
print    "Dereference    anonymous    array    stored    at    2nd    index:    ",
"@{$two_dimen_array -> [2]}","\n";
print "Dereference and get the value stored at 0th index : ", $two_dimen_array
-> [2][0],"\n";
print "Dereference and get the value stored at 1st index : ", $two_dimen_array
-> [2]->[1],"\n";
print "\n";
print "Print as a matrix:\n";
foreach my $main_array (@{$two_dimen_array})
{
        foreach my $inner_arrays (@{$main_array})
        {
        print "$inner_arrays\t";
        }
print "\n";
}
```

Output:
Reference: ARRAY(0x1e27a04)
Dereference $two_dimen_array:
ARRAY(0x477b94) ARRAY(0x1e0b774) ARRAY(0x1e0b864)

Dereference anonymous array stored at 0th index: 1 2 3
Dereference and get the value stored at 0th index : 1
Dereference and get the value stored at 1st index : 2

Dereference anonymous array stored at 2nd index: 7 8 9
Dereference and get the value stored at 0th index : 7
Dereference and get the value stored at 1st index : 8

Print as a matrix:
1   2   3
4   5   6
7   8   9

Explanation: A two dimensional array is created which is itself an array of arrays. In the statement

> my $two_dimen_array = [[1, 2, 3], [4, 5, 6], [7, 8, 9]];
>
> one anonymous array has been created whose each index contain another anonymous array. Therefore nested loops have been used to access all values of outer and inner anonymous arrays. The outer loop works for the main anonymous array while the inner loop works for main array indexes which itself contains three anonymous arrays.

Points to remember

- A reference is a scalar value which represents the memory location of the referent.
- The function ref is used to know the type of referent.
- Anonymous array and associative array can be created by using [ ] and { }, respectively.
- References help to create complex data structures including array of arrays, hash of arrays.

Test Yourself

1. Write a program to create reference of an array and dereference it.
2. Write a program to print the value associated with a key of associative array using its reference.
3. Write a program to create reference of a reference.
4. Write a program to print a 3 * 3 matrix.

Find errors

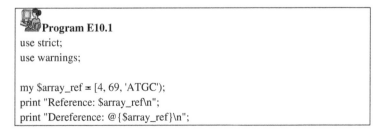

Program E10.1
```
use strict;
use warnings;

my $array_ref = [4, 69, 'ATGC');
print "Reference: $array_ref\n";
print "Dereference: @{$array_ref}\n";
```

Output:
Error messsage

Program E10.2
```
use strict;
use warnings;

my $scalar = 100;
print "Scalar Value: $scalar\n";
my $scalar_ref = \$scalar;
print "Reference1: $scalar_ref\n";

my $scalar_ref1 = \$scalar_ref;
print "Reference2: $scalar_ref1\n";

print "Dereference \$scalar_ref: $scalar_ref\n";
print "Dereference \$scalar_ref1: ", $$scalar_ref1,"\n";
```

Output:
Scalar Value: 100
Reference1: SCALAR(0x4434ec)
Reference2: REF(0x4435c4)
Dereference $scalar_ref: SCALAR(0x4434ec) #undesired output
Dereference $scalar_ref1: SCALAR(0x4434ec) #undesired output

Chapter 11

Subroutines

Subroutines are user defined functions. The advantage of creating subroutine is to reduce the duplication of code in the program. In case, a particular task has to be repeated again and again in the program and any in-built function is unable to do the task, then it is not good to copy the same chunk of code at several places in the same program. Instead, if a custom made function (subroutine) is created the subroutine call will perform the required task without code duplication. To create a subroutine a keyword sub followed by subroutine name and code block is used, generally at the end of program.

sub Subroutine_Name
{
Subroutine code block;
}

A subroutine call sends a request for the execution of that specific chunk of code.

Subroutine_Name( ); # subroutine call
&Subroutine_Name( ); # subroutine call

Values stored in a variable can be passed to a subroutine as an argument in the form of a list. The argument list passes to a subroutine through a special @_ array. Similar to most of the functions of Perl, subroutines also returns a value using the function return. The return function takes the argument and passes it to the main program from where subroutine is called. The returned value can be assigned to a variable in the main program for further use.

Program 11.1

```
# Program to add two numbers using subroutine
#Main program
use strict;
use warnings;

add(4,6); #Subroutine call
&add(6,1); #Subroutine call

#Subroutine definition
sub add
{
print "Values passed to subroutine through \@_ : @_\n";
my ($first, $second) = @_;

my $sum = $first + $second;
print "Sum is: $sum\n\n";
}
```

Output:
Values passed to subroutine through @_ : 4 6
Sum is: 10

Values passed to subroutine through @_ : 6 1
Sum is: 7

Explanation: In the main program the subroutine is called twice and arguments are passed as a list. The arguments pass to subroutine through @_ array. The 0th index $_[0] of @_ holds the first argument and the 1st index $_[1] of @_ holds the second argument. Inside the subroutine these arguments are assigned to scalar variables for addition.

Program 11.2

```perl
# Program to add two numbers using subroutine and return the value
use strict;
use warnings;

my $sum_first = add(4,6); #Subroutine call
my $sum_second = &add(6,1); #Subroutine call

print "The sum of 4 and 6 is: $sum_first\n";
print "The sum of 6 and 1 is: $sum_second \n";

#Subroutine definition
sub add
{
my $first = shift(@_);
my $second = shift(@_);
my $sum = $first + $second;
return($sum);
}
```

Output:
The sum of 4 and 6 is: 10
The sum of 6 and 1 is: 7

Explanation: The arguments are passed to the subroutine through @_ therefore shift function is used to get those arguments. After addition the value is returned to the main program where the returned value is stored in scalar variable and further used in print function.

Program 11.3

```perl
# Program to pass array to subroutine
use strict;
use warnings;

my @array = qw (1 3 5 6 8);
array(@array); #Subroutine call
```

```
#Subroutine definition
sub array
{
my @array_sub = @_;
print "Array values: @array_sub\n";
}
```

Output:
Array values: 1 3 5 6 8

Program 11.4
```
# Program to pass two arrays to subroutine
use strict;
use warnings;

my @fruits = qw (Apple Banana Grapes);
my @color = qw (Red Yellow Green);
array(@fruits, @color); #Subroutine call

#Subroutine definition
sub array
{
print "Values in \@_ : @_\n";
my (@fruits_sub,@color_sub) = @_;
print "\@fruits_sub values: @fruits_sub\n";
print "\@color_sub values: @color_sub\n";
}
```

Output:
Values in @_ : Apple Banana Grapes Red Yellow Green
@fruits_sub values: Apple Banana Grapes Red Yellow Green
@color_sub values:

Explanation: Since subroutine passes the arguments as a list therefore when two arrays are provided as an argument in the subroutine call they get flattened into @_ inside the subroutine and assigned to array @fruits_sub.

Program 11.5
```
# Program to pass two arrays to subroutine as reference
use strict;
use warnings;

my @fruits = qw (Apple Banana Grapes);
my @color = qw (Red Yellow Green);
array(\@fruits, \@color); #Subroutine call

#Subroutine definition
sub array
{
print "Values in \@_ : @_\n";
my ($fruits, $color) = @_;
print "\@fruits values: @{$fruits}\n";
print "\@color values: @{$color}\n";
}
```

Output:
Values in @_ : ARRAY(0x1d634a4) ARRAY(0x1d634d4)
@fruits values: Apple Banana Grapes
@color values: Red Yellow Green

Explanation: It is convenient to pass multiple arrays as a reference to a subroutine. Since a reference is a scalar quantity which can be easily assigned to a scalar variable inside subroutine. The variable holding the reference of array can be dereferenced to get the array elements.

Program 11.6
```
# Program to pass associative array to subroutine
use strict;
use warnings;
```

```
my %Gene_length = ( 'MDR', 2400,'BRAC', 2268,'Rubisco', 1800) ;

asso_array(%Gene_length); #Subroutine call

#Subroutine definition
sub asso_array
{
my %asso_array_sub = @_;
print "Associative array key->values: ", %asso_array_sub,"\n";
}
```

Output:

Associative array key->values: MDR2400BRAC2268Rubisco1800

Program 11.7

```
# Program to pass two associative arrays to subroutine
use strict;
use warnings;

my %Gene_length = ( 'MDR', 2400,'BRAC', 2268,'Rubisco', 1800) ;
my %Protein_length = ( 'MDR_P', 800,'BRAC_P', 756,'Rubisco_P', 600) ;
asso_array (%Gene_length, %Protein_length); #Subroutine call

#Subroutine definition
sub asso_array
{
print "Values in \@_ : @_\n";
my (%Gene_length_sub,%Protein_length_sub) = @_;
print "Key->Values for \%Gene_length_sub: ", %Gene_length_sub,"\n";
print "Key->Values for \%Protein_length_sub: ", %Protein_length_sub,"\n";
}
```

Output:

Values in @_ : MDR 2400 BRAC 2268 Rubisco 1800 MDR_P 800 Rubisco_P 600 BRAC_P 756
Key->Values for %Gene_length_sub:
Rubisco_P600MDR_P800BRAC_P756MDR2400Rubisco1800BRAC2268
Key->Values for %Protein_length_sub:

Explanation: Since subroutines pass the arguments as a list therefore when two associative arrays are provided as an argument in the subroutine call they get flattened into @_ inside the subroutine and assigned to %Gene_length_sub.

Program 11.8

```
# Program to pass two associative arrays to subroutine as reference
use strict;
use warnings;

my %Gene_length = ( 'MDR', 2400,'BRAC', 2268,'Rubisco', 1800) ;
my %Protein_length = ( 'MDR_P', 800,'BRAC_P', 756,'Rubisco_P', 600) ;
asso_array (\%Gene_length, \%Protein_length); #Subroutine call

#Subroutine definition
sub asso_array
{
print "Values in \@_ : @_\n";
my ($Gene_length,$Protein_length) = @_;
print "\%Gene_length Key->Values: ", %{$Gene_length},"\n";
print "\%Protein_length Key->Values: ", %{$Protein_length},"\n";
}
```

Output:
Values in @_ : HASH(0x6334a4) HASH(0x633504)
%Gene_length Key->Values: BRAC2268MDR2400Rubisco1800
%Protein_length Key->Values: MDR_P800Rubisco_P600BRAC_P756

Explanation: It is convenient to pass multiple associative arrays as a reference to a subroutine. Since a reference is a scalar quantity which can be easily assigned to a scalar variable inside subroutine. The variable holding the reference of associative array can be dereferenced to get the key-value pairs.

Points to remember

- Subroutines are user defined functions.
- It helps to create a function according to user's requirement.
- Arguments are passed to a subroutine using @_ array.
- It is better to pass multiple arrays or associative arrays as references to a subroutine.

Test Yourself

1. Write a program to create a subroutine to print a table of a number provided as an argument.
2. Create a subroutine to count the characters in a string.
3. Write a program to find a pattern passed as an argument to subroutine.
4. Write a program to swap values of two equal sized arrays using subroutine.

Find errors

Program E11.1
```
use strict;
use warnings;

my $sum = add(4,6);
print "The sum of 4 and 6 is: $sum\n";

sub add
{
my $first = shift(@_);
my $second;
my $sum = $first + $second;
return($sum);
}
```

Output:
The sum of 4 and 6 is: 4 # Undesired output

Program E11.2

```perl
use strict;
use warnings;

my @fruits = qw (Apple Banana Grapes);
my @color = qw (Red Yellow Green);
array(@fruits, \@color);

sub array
{
print "Values in \@_ : @_\n";
my ($fruits, $color) = @_;
print "\@fruits values: @{$fruits}\n";
print "\@color values: @{$color}\n";
}
```

Output:
Undesired output

Chapter 12

File and Directory Handling

In bioinformatics dealing with huge amount of data is a common task. A complete genome sequence from an analysis pipeline constitutes big data. It is convenient to deal with such files in an automated manner. File handling allows performing automatic manipulation of huge data by dealing with files. A file can be opened in three modes:

Mode	Symbol	Description
Read	<	Only read the content of file
Write	>	Creates a new file
Append	>>	Append data in the already existing file

To open a file in the read mode the following statement is used

open(FILEHANDLE, "<FILE_NAME");

To create a new file

open(FILEHANDLE, ">FILE_NAME");

To append data in already existing file

open(FILEHANDLE, ">>FILE_NAME");

The file handle takes the control of the file in any of these modes. Sometimes all the files of a directory have to be opened to do a task. For example, a genome may consist of multiple chromosomes and each chromosome sequence is stored in a separate file within a directory. If a pattern has to be located in all these chromosomes in automatic manner directory handling will be useful along with file handling. To open a directory the following statement is used

opendir(DIRHANDLE, DIRNAME);

along with readdir function which reads the directory content using directory handle.

Program 12.1
```perl
# Program to open a file and read the contents
use strict;
use warnings;

my @inFile;
if(open(IN,"<Triticum.fasta")) #< optional
{
@inFile = <IN>;
print "File found\n\n";
close(IN);
}
else{
print "File not found\n";
}
print "Content of file:\n\n";
foreach my $line (@inFile)
{
print $line;
}
```

Input File: Triticum.fasta
>gi|14017554|rcf|NP_114241.1| ribosomal protein S16 [Triticum aestivum]
MLKLRLKRCGRKQQAVYRIVAIDVRSRREGRDLRKVGFYDPIKNQTC
LNVPAILYFLEKGAQPTRTVYDI
LRKAEFFKEKESTLS
>gi|14017555|ref|NP_114242.1| photosystem II protein K [Triticum aestivum]
MPNILSLTCICFNSVIYPTSFFFAKLPEAYAIFNPIVDFMPVIPLFFFLLAF

VWQAAVSFR
>gi|14017556|ref|NP_114243.1| photosystem II protein I [Triticum aestivum]
MLTLKLFVYTVVIFFVSLFIFGFLSNDPGRNPGREE

Output:
File found
Content of file:

>gi|14017554|ref|NP_114241.1| ribosomal protein S16 [Triticum aestivum]
MLKLRLKRCGRKQQAVYRIVAIDVRSRREGRDLRKVGFYDPIKNQTC
LNVPAILYFLEKGAQPTRTVYDI
LRKAEFFKEKESTLS
>gi|14017555|ref|NP_114242.1| photosystem II protein K [Triticum aestivum]
MPNILSLTCICFNSVIYPTSFFFAKLPEAYAIFNPIVDFMPVIPLFFFLLAF
VWQAAVSFR
>gi|14017556|ref|NP_114243.1| photosystem II protein I [Triticum aestivum]
MLTLKLFVYTVVIFFVSLFIFGFLSNDPGRNPGREE

Explanation: The open statement is used as an expression in if statement just to get the message whether file found or not. If file opens the control structure if evaluates to be true otherwise not. IN is used as a file handle using which all the contents of the file have been stored in an array through standard input. Close is used to close the file handle. All the file data have been stored in the array, one line of the file in each index of array, therefore a foreach loop is used to iterate over all indexes of array to get the file data.

Notice that the file handling output depends on the file used as an input.

Program 12.2
Program to open a file and read the contents line by line
use strict;
use warnings;

my $inFile; #Variable to hold input data from file
open(IN,"Triticum.fasta") || die "File not found";
print "Content of file:\n\n";
while ($inFile = <IN>)
{

```
print "$inFile";
}
close(IN);
```

Output:
Content of file:

>gi|14017554|ref|NP_114241.1| ribosomal protein S16 [Triticum aestivum]
MLKLRLKRCGRKQQAVYRIVAIDVRSRREGRDLRKVGFYDPIKNQTC
LNVPAILYFLEKGAQPTRTVYDI
LRKAEFFKEKESTLS
>gi|14017555|ref|NP_114242.1| photosystem II protein K [Triticum aestivum]
MPNILSLTCICFNSVIYPTSFFFAKLPEAYAIFNPIVDFMPVIPLFFFLLAF
VWQAAVSFR
>gi|14017556|ref|NP_114243.1| photosystem II protein I [Triticum aestivum]
MLTLKLFVYTVVIFFVSLFIFGFLSNDPGRNPGREE

Explanation: The open statement is used along with || (OR) operator. In case the script is unable to find the file then the die function terminates the program with the message. IN is used as a file handle using which all the contents of the file have been read through standard input in a while loop. The lines of the file have been read line by line instead of storing all data of file in the array as in previous program. Close is used to close the file handle.

Program 12.3
```
# Program to open a file stored in another directory
use strict;
use warnings;

my $inFile; #Variable to hold input data from file
open(IN,"D:/Sequence/Triticum.fasta") || die "File not found";

print "Content of file:\n\n";
while ($inFile = <IN>)
{
print "$inFile";
}
close(IN);
```

Output:
Content of file:

>gil14017554lreflNP_114241.1l ribosomal protein S16 [Triticum aestivum]
MLKLRLKRCGRKQQAVYRIVAIDVRSRREGRDLRKVGFYDPIKNQTC
LNVPAILYFLEKGAQPTRTVYDI
LRKAEFFKEKESTLS
>gil14017555lreflNP_114242.1l photosystem II protein K [Triticum aestivum]
MPNILSLTCICFNSVIYPTSFFFAKLPEAYAIFNPIVDFMPVIPLFFFLLAF
VWQAAVSFR
>gil14017556lreflNP_114243.1l photosystem II protein I [Triticum aestivum]
MLTLKLFVYTVVIFFVSLFIFGFLSNDPGRNPGREE

Explanation: If the file to be opened is not present in the same directory (folder) where the Perl program is present, provide the complete path where the file is stored along with file name in the open statement.

Program 12.4
Program to open a file and write its contents in new file
use strict;
use warnings;

my $inFile = 'Triticum.fasta'; #Variable to hold input file name
my $outFile = 'Triticum.New.fasta'; #Variable to hold output file name
my $fileData; #Variable to hold input data from file
open(IN,"$inFile") Il die "File not found";
open(OUT,">$outFile") Il die "New file not created";

print "Content of file:\n\n";
while ($fileData = <IN>)
{
print "$fileData"; #print on command prompt
print OUT "$fileData"; #print in new file
}
close(IN);
close(OUT);

Output:
Content of file:

>gi|14017554|ref|NP_114241.1| ribosomal protein S16 [Triticum aestivum]
MLKLRLKRCGRKQQAVYRIVAIDVRSRREGRDLRKVGFYDPIKNQTC
LNVPAILYFLEKGAQPTRTVYDI
LRKAEFFKEKESTLS
>gi|14017555|ref|NP_114242.1| photosystem II protein K [Triticum aestivum]
MPNILSLTCICFNSVIYPTSFFFAKLPEAYAIFNPIVDFMPVIPLFFFLLAF
VWQAAVSFR
>gi|14017556|ref|NP_114243.1| photosystem II protein I [Triticum aestivum]
MLTLKLFVYTVVIFFVSLFIFGFLSNDPGRNPGREE

Explanation: The first open command with IN file handle opens the file in read mode. The second open command with OUT file handle opens a new file in write mode. While loop reads the data line by line using IN file handle whereas the print statement with OUT file handle writes the data into new file. If the file with the same name as $outFile is already present with data in it, entire data has been erased and new data has been written to it. Beware the old data of the file will be vanished and the file contains only newly written data.

Program 12.5

```
# Program to open a file and write its contents in existing file
use strict;
use warnings;

my $inFile = 'Triticum.fasta'; #Variable to hold input file name
my $outFile = 'Triticum.New.fasta'; #Variable to hold output file name
my $fileData; #Variable to hold input data from file
open(IN,"$inFile") || die "File not found";
open(APPEND,">>$outFile") || die "New file not created"; #>> append mode

print "Content of file:\n\n";
while ($fileData = <IN>)
{
print "$fileData"; #print on command prompt
```

```
print APPEND "$fileData"; #print in new file
}
close(IN);
close(APPEND);
```

Output:
Content of file:

```
>gi|14017554|ref|NP_114241.1| ribosomal protein S16 [Triticum aestivum]
MLKLRLKRCGRKQQAVYRIVAIDVRSRREGRDLRKVGFYDPIKNQTC
LNVPAILYFLEKGAQPTRTVYDI
LRKAEFFKEKESTLS
>gi|14017555|ref|NP_114242.1| photosystem II protein K [Triticum aestivum]
MPNILSLTCICFNSVIYPTSFFFAKLPEAYAIFNPIVDFMPVIPLFFFLLAF
VWQAAVSFR
>gi|14017556|ref|NP_114243.1| photosystem II protein I [Triticum aestivum]
MLTLKLFVYTVVIFFVSLFIFGFLSNDPGRNPGREE
```

Explanation: The first open command with IN file handle opens the file in read mode. The second open command with OUT file handle opens an existing file in append mode. While loop reads the data line by line using IN file handle whereas the print statement with APPEND file handle writes the data into existing file. The newly written data gets appended with the old data of the file and the file contains both old data as well as newly written data.

Program 12.6

```
# Program to open a directory and get the file names
use strict;
use warnings;

my $dirPath = "D:/Sequence";
opendir(DIR,$dirPath) or die "Can't find $dirPath: $!";

print "Name of files present in Sequence directory:\n";

while (defined(my $file = readdir(DIR)))
{
print "$file\n";
```

```
}
close(DIR);
```

Output:
Name of files present in Sequence directory:

.

..

Marchantia.fasta
Oryza.fasta
Triticum.fasta

Explanation: The opendir function uses a directory handle to take the control of specified directory. The readdir function then reads all the file names from the directory using directory handle DIR. The readdir function is used as an expression to defined function which itself is used as an expression to while loop. The readdir function takes one filename and assign it to the $file variable. The defined function evaluates whether $file contains a defined value if yes the while evaluates to be true and it prints the file name stored in $file. In this way the readdir function iterates over all the file names present in the directory. Notice a . and .. in the output. The single dot represents the current directory and the .. represents the parent directory.

Program 12.7
```
# Program to open a directory and get the relevant file names
use strict;
use warnings;

my $dirPath = "D:/Sequence";
opendir(DIR,$dirPath) or die "Can't find $dirPath: $!";
my @filenames; #Array to store all relevant file names from directory
while (defined(my $file = readdir(DIR)))
{
next if $file =~ /^\.\.?/;
#the names of files present in dir assigned to an array
push(@filenames,$file);
}
```

148

```
close(DIR);
print "Name of files present in Sequence directory:\n";
foreach my $filename (@filenames)
{
print "$filename\n";
}
```

Output:
Name of files present in Sequence directory:
Marchantia.fasta
Oryza.fasta
Triticum.fasta

Explanation: The opendir function uses a directory handle to take the control of specified directory. The readdir function then reads all the file names from the directory using directory handle DIR. The readdir function is used as an expression to defined function which itself is used as an expression to while loop. The readdir function takes one filename and assign it to the $file variable. The defined function evaluates whether $file contains a defined value if yes the while evaluates to be true and moves to its code block. The $file name is matched with a . or .. at first position itself. A ^ looks for a pattern in the beginning of line and a ? quantify the pattern as {0, 1}. This regular expression looks for a . or .. in the beginning of line. In case the beginning of line is not specified to find a . none of the file names appear in the output since the regular expression matches a . in the file extension and next statement gets executed. If regular expression finds a . or .. in the beginning the control structure if evaluates to be true and next statement gets executed. Therefore the loop moves to next iteration without pushing the value of $file to array. In this way the readdir function iterates over all the file names present in the directory. The . and .. are skipped and only relevant file names are pushed in the array @filenames.

Program 12.8

```perl
# Program to open a directory and read the contents of all files one by one
use strict;
use warnings;


my $dirPath = "D:/Sequence";
opendir(DIR,$dirPath) or die "Can't find $dirPath: $!";


while (defined(my $file = readdir(DIR)))
{
next if $file =~ /^\.\.?/;


open(IN,"$dirPath/$file") || die "File not found";
print "\n\nContent of file $file:\n\n";
        while (my $fileData = <IN>)
        {
        print "$fileData"; #print on command prompt
        }
        close(IN);
}
close(DIR);
```

Output:
Content of file Marchantia.fasta:

>gi|11466674|ref|NP_039270.1| hypothetical protein MapoCp001 [Marchantia polymorpha]
TTTPKKPNSALRKIARVRLTSGFEITAYIPGIGHNLQEHSVVLVRGGRV
KDLPGVRYHIIRGTLDAVGVK
DRQQGRSKYGVKKSK
>gi|11466675|ref|NP_039271.1| ribosomal   protein   S7   [Marchantia polymorpha]
MSRKSIAEKQVAKPDPIYRNRLVNMLVNRILKNGKKSLAYRILYKAM
KNIKQKTKKNPLFVLRQAVRKVT
PNVTVKARRIDGSTYQVPLEIKSTQGKALAIRWLLGASRKRSGQNMAF
KLSYELIDAARDNGIAIRKKEE
THKMAEANRAFAHFR
>gi|11466676|ref|NP_039272.1| NADH dehydrogenase subunit 2 [Marchantia polymorpha]
MKLELDMFFLYGSTILPECILIFSLLIILIIDLTFPKKDTIWLYFISLTSLLIS
IIILLFQYKTDPIISF
LGSFQTDSFNRIFQSFIVFCSILCIPLSIEYIKCAKMAIPEFLIFILTATVGG

MFLCGANDLVTIFVSLE
CLSLCSYLLCGYTKRDIRSNEAAIKYLLIGGTSSSILAYGFSWLYGLSG
GETNIQKITNGLLNAETYNSS
GTFIAFICILVGLAFKLSLVPFHQWTPDIYEGSPTPVVAFLSVTSKIAGL
ALATRILNILFSFSPNEWKI
FLEILAILSMILGNLVAITQTSMKRMLAYSSISQIGYILIGLITGDLKGYT
SMTIYVFFYIFMNLGTFAC
IILYSLRTGTDNIRDYAGLYIKDPLLSFSLTLCLLSLGGLPPLTGFFGKLY
LFWCGWQSGFYLLVFIALI
TSVISLYYYLKIIKLILTKKNNEINPYIQAYIITSPTFFSKNPIEFVMIFCVL
GSTFLGIIINPIFSFFQ
DSLSLSVFFIK
>gi|11466677|ref|NP_039273.1| photosystem II M protein [Marchantia polymorpha]
MEVNILAFIATALFILIPTAFLLILYVQTASQNS
>gi|11466678|ref|NP_039274.1| hypothetical protein MapoCp005 [Marchantia polymorpha]
MNHMELGPSTILGVGLIIIGLFLYALKLREPYVSRDYDFFFSCIGLLCGG
ILFFQGWRLDPILLLSQILL
SGTTIFFIAESLYLRKNLNFVKSKKKYINLAKKNIYKYIYENFKLKKKW
NELNYTRHIFYKKKKH

Content of file Oryza.fasta:

>gi|109156639|ref|YP_654258.1| ribosomal protein S15 [Oryza sativa Indica Group]

MKKKGGRKIFGFMVKEEKEENWGSVEFQVFSFTNKIRRLASHLELHK
KDFSSERGLRRLLGKRQRLLAYL
AKKNRVRYKKLISQLDIRER
>gi|112113314|ref|YP_654259.2| ribosomal protein S7 [Oryza sativa Indica Group]
MSRRGTAEKRTAKSDPIFRNRLVNMVVNRIMKDGKKSLAYQILYRAV
KKIQQKTETNPLLVLRQAIRRVT
PNIGVKTRRNKKGSTRKVPIEIGSKQGRALAIRWLLEASQKRPGRNMA
FKLSSELVDAAKGGGGAIRKKE
ATHRMAEANRALAHFR
>gi|109156641|ref|YP_654260.1| ribosomal protein L23 [Oryza sativa Indica Group]

MDGIKYAVFTEKSLRLLGKNQYTFNVESGFTKTEIKHWVELFFGVKV
VAVNSHRLPGKGRRMGPILGHTM
HYRRMIITLQPGYSIPLLDREKN

>gi|109156642|ref|YP_654261.1| ribosomal protein L2 [Oryza sativa Indica Group]
MIHGRHRCGKGRNSRGIITARHRGGGHKRLYRKIDFRRNQKDISGRIV
TIEYDPNRNAYICLIHYGDGEK
GYILHPRGAIIGDTIVSGTKVPISMGNALPLSAV
>gi|127711708|ref|YP_001095993.1| ribosomal protein S19 [Oryza sativa Indica Gro
up]
MTRKKTNPFVAHHLLAKIEKVNMKEEKETIVTWSRASSILPAMVGHTI
AIHNGKEHIPIYITNPMVGRKL
GEFVPTRHFTSYESARKDTKSRR

Content of file Triticum.fasta:

>gi|14017554|ref|NP_114241.1| ribosomal protein S16 [Triticum aestivum]
MLKLRLKRCGRKQQAVYRIVAIDVRSRREGRDLRKVGFYDPIKNQTC
LNVPAILYFLEKGAQPTRTVYDI
LRKAEFFKEKESTLS
>gi|14017555|ref|NP_114242.1| photosystem II protein K [Triticum aestivum]
MPNILSLTCICFNSVIYPTSFFFAKLPEAYAIFNPIVDFMPVIPLFFFLLAF
VWQAAVSFR
>gi|14017556|ref|NP_114243.1| photosystem II protein I [Triticum aestivum]
MLTLKLFVYTVVIFFVSLFIFGFLSNDPGRNPGREE

Explanation: The directory handling is used to open the directory and filenames fetched using readdir. To read the file contents the file handling is used only on relevant file names. The nested while loops are used in this program. The outer while loop iterates over filenames using readdir whereas the inner while loop iterates over file data using file handle.

Points to remember

- Three modes (read, write and append) are used to deal with a file.
- A file handle is used to control a file.
- The < sign is used to open a file. However it is optional.
- A > sign is used for read mode while >> sign for append mode.
- The directory handle controls the directory.

Test Yourself

1. Write a program to open a file and print it contents.
2. Write a program to print a 3 * 3 matrix in a new file.
3. Write a program to count number of fasta formatted sequences in a file.
4. Write a program to copy the content of multiple files into a single file.

Find errors

Program E12.1
use strict;
use warnings;

```
my @inFile;
if(open(IN,"Triticum.fasta"))
{
$inFile = <IN>;
print "File found\n\n";
close(IN);
}
else{
print "File not found\n";
}
print "Content of file:\n\n";
foreach my $line (@inFile)
{
print $line;
}
```

Output:
File found

Content of file: # Undesired output

Program E12.2
use strict;
use warnings;

```
my $inFile = 'Triticum.fasta';
```

153

```
my $outFile = 'Triticum.New.fasta';
my $fileData;
open(IN,"$inFile") || die "File not found";
open(OUT,"$outFile") || die "New file not created";

while ($fileData = <IN>)
{
print OUT "$fileData";
}
close(IN);
```

Output:

New file not created ...

Chapter 13

Modules and Packages

A module gives the flexibility to reuse the code again and again without duplicating the code in different programs. Often a particular subroutine is so useful that it is used in most of the programs. One way to use the subroutine is to copy the code in every program that leads to redundancy of code in all the programs. The better way is to create a module and write the subroutine inside the module. Whenever the subroutine is required in a program just use the module in the program and all the code including the subroutine from module becomes available to the program. This helps in removing the redundancy of code in programs. A module contains the Perl code and is created by saving the file with .pm extension. The last line of a module ends with a 1 followed by a semicolon (1;) just to know whether module is loaded properly in your main program during execution.

Program 13.1

```
# Program to generate complementary DNA
#  using subroutine from a module
use strict;
use warnings;

use seq;
my $DNA = 'CGATCGTAGCTAGCGACGATGC';
print "$DNA \t #DNA Sequence\n";
my $DNA_complement = complementary($DNA);
print "$DNA_complement \t #Complementary DNA Sequence\n";
```

Module: seq.pm
```
#subroutine to generate complementary DNA sequence
sub complementary
{
my $seq = shift;
$seq =~ tr/ATGC/TACG/;
return($seq);
}
1;
```

Output:
CGATCGTAGCTAGCGACGATGC #DNA Sequence
GCTAGCATCGATCGCTGCTACG #Complementary DNA Sequence

Explanation: A text file is created with a subroutine to generate complementary DNA sequence and saved with seq.pm name to classify it as a module. Notice the presence of 1; at the end of module. This module is used in the main program with the statement **use seq**. The module code is not duplicated in the program instead it is just used. There is no subroutine in the main program still it generates a complementary DNA sequence using module's subroutine. This is the reusability of the code.

Program 13.2
```
# Program to generate complementary DNA using module stored in a
directory
use strict;
use warnings;

use modules::sequence;
my $DNA = 'CGATCGTAGCTAGCGACGATGC';
print "$DNA \t #DNA Sequence\n";
my $DNA_complement = complementary($DNA);
print "$DNA_complement \t #Complementary DNA Sequence\n";
```

Module: sequence.pm
#subroutine to generate complementary DNA sequence

```
sub complementary
{
my $seq = shift;
$seq =~ tr/ATGC/TACG/;
return($seq);
}
1;
```

Output:
CGATCGTAGCTAGCGACGATGC   #DNA Sequence
GCTAGCATCGATCGCTGCTACG   #Complementary DNA Sequence

Explanation: In case the module is not stored in the directory where main program is stored then provide the module's directory name along with module name in the use statement. In this program the statement

use modules::sequence;

includes a module name (sequence) along with the directory name (modules) where sequence module is stored.

Packages

A package creates a separate namespace during the execution of program. A namespace consists of a table called name table created in memory which records names of all variables and subroutines of that program. The names of variables and subroutines in the name table point towards the memory where the values or the codes are located. Multiple namespaces can be created and used in Perl. The statement

package PackageName;

creates a new namespace and all variables and subroutines after PackageName becomes the part of namespace called PackageName. Generally a package is defined with a module. Moreover the name of the package should be same as the module name to avoid ambiguity. In case a subroutine with the same name is present in the main program and also in the module in which a package is created there is no confusion whether the subroutine is called from main program or from module.

Program 13.3

```perl
# Program to generate complementary DNA and RNA sequence
# using same subroutine name
use strict;
use warnings;

use modules::sequence;
my $DNA = 'CGATCGTAGCTAGCGACGATGC';
print "$DNA \t #DNA Sequence\n";

my $DNA_complement = complement($DNA);
print "$DNA_complement \t #Wrong DNA complement\n\n";

my $DNA_complement = sequence::complement($DNA);
print "$DNA \t #DNA Sequence\n";
print "$DNA_complement \t #Correct DNA complement\n\n";

my $RNA = 'AUGCAGUCGUAGCAUCUACGUC';
my $RNA_complement = complement($RNA);
print "$RNA \t #RNA Sequence\n";
print "$RNA_complement \t #Complementary RNA Sequence\n";

sub complement
{
my $seq = shift;
$seq =~ tr/AUGC/UACG/; #Complementary RNA
return($seq);
}
```

Module: sequence.pm
package sequence;

```perl
#subroutine to generate complementary DNA sequence
sub complement
{
my $seq = shift;
$seq =~ tr/ATGC/TACG/;
return($seq);
}
1;
```

Output:

```
CGATCGTAGCTAGCGACGATGC   #DNA Sequence
GCUTGCTUCGTUCGCUGCUTCG   #Wrong DNA complement

CGATCGTAGCTAGCGACGATGC   #DNA Sequence
GCTAGCATCGATCGCTGCTACG   #Correct DNA complement

AUGCAGUCGUAGCAUCUACGUC   #RNA Sequence
UACGUCAGCAUCGUAGAUGCAG   #Complementary RNA Sequence
```

Explanation: A module is created with a package (namespace) named sequence. The module contains a subroutine named complement, to generate complementary DNA sequence, whereas the main program also contains a subroutine with same name, however, to generate complementary RNA sequence. When the subroutine complement is called on DNA sequence

my $DNA_complement = complement($DNA);

it calls the subroutine from main program which is to generate complementary RNA sequence. Consequently the wrong DNA complement has been generated. Another statement

my $DNA_complement = sequence::complement($DNA);

uses the package sequence along with the subroutine call and a correct DNA complement has been generated. Therefore by using the package name it is clear whether the subroutine has to be called from main program or from module.

Points to remember

- Modules provide the flexibility to reuse the code.
- A module always ends with 1; to mark the end of module.
- Always save the module files with .pm extension.
- Use the same name for a package and module.

Test Yourself

1. Write a program to create a module with subroutine to find a pattern. Call the subroutine in main program.

2. Write a program to convert three letter amino acid codes to one letter codes using a subroutine from a module.

3. Write a program to find open reading frame in a coding sequence using subroutine named ORF from a module.

4. Write a program to generate complement of RNA sequence using a subroutine named complement from a module. Generate complement of DNA sequence using the same subroutine name from main program.

Find errors

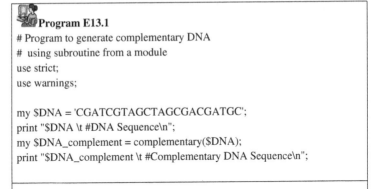

Program E13.1
```
# Program to generate complementary DNA
#  using subroutine from a module
use strict;
use warnings;

my $DNA = 'CGATCGTAGCTAGCGACGATGC';
print "$DNA \t #DNA Sequence\n";
my $DNA_complement = complementary($DNA);
print "$DNA_complement \t #Complementary DNA Sequence\n";
```

Module: seq.pm
```
#subroutine to generate complementary DNA sequence
sub complementary
{
my $seq = shift;
$seq =~ tr/ATGC/TACG/;
return($seq);
}
1;
```

Output:

CGATCGTAGCTAGCGACGATGC   #DNA Sequence
Undefined subroutine &main::complementary called at ......

**Program E13.2**
use strict;
use warnings;

use modules::sequence;
my $DNA = 'CGATCGTAGCTAGCGACGATGC';
print "$DNA \t #DNA Sequence\n";
my $DNA_complement = complement($DNA);
print "$DNA_complement \t #Complementary DNA Sequence\n";

Module: sequence.pm
package sequence;

#subroutine to generate complementary DNA sequence
sub complement
{
my $seq = shift;
$seq =~ tr/ATGC/TACG/;
return($seq);
}
1;

Output:

CGATCGTAGCTAGCGACGATGC   #DNA Sequence
Undefined subroutine &main::complement called at ...

Find errors: Solutions

Chapter 1

Program E1.1

#My first Perl program
print "Hello there";   # " missing

Output:
Hello there

Program E1.2

#My first Perl program
print "Hello there";   #P in capital letter

Output:
Hello there

Chapter 2

Program E2.1

```
use strict;
use warnings;

my $gene_seq = "ATGCTGCAGCTAGGCATGCTAGC" ;

print "$gene_seq"; #missing $
```

Output:
ATGCTGCAGCTAGGCATGCTAGC

Program E2.2

```
use strict;
use warnings;

my $accession_number = "NC_43210"; #missing semicolon

print "$accession_number";
```

Output:
NC_43210

Chapter 3

Program E3.1
use strict;
use warnings;

print "Enter a number = ";
my $number = <stdin>; #missing >
print "Number = $number";

Output:
Enter a number = 6
Number = 6

Program E3.2
use strict;
use warnings;

print "Enter first number = ";
my $first_number = <stdin>;
chop($first_number);
print "Enter second number = ";
my $second_number = <stdin>;
chop($second_number); # **chop($first_number);**
my $sum = $first_number + $second_number;
print "The sum of numbers is = $sum";

Output:
Enter first number = 4
Enter second number = 4
The sum of numbers is = 8

Chapter 4

Program E4.1

```
use strict;
use warnings;

my @array = ('A','book','on','perl')  ; #missing ,
print "Array of strings\n";
print "@array","\n\n";
```

Output:
Array of strings
A book on perl

Program E4.2

```
use strict;
use warnings;

my @genes = ('MDR1', 'BRAC1')  ;
print "Value in last index: $genes[$#genes]\n"; # $ missing
```

Output:
Value in last index: BRAC1

Chapter 5

Program E5.1
use strict;
use warnings;

my %Gene_length = ('MDR' => 2400,'BRAC' => 2267,'Rubisco' => 1700) ; #
> missing from =>
print "Key-value pairs in associative array: ",%Gene_length,"\n";

Output:
Key-value pairs in associative array: BRAC2267MDR2400Rubisco1700

Program E5.2
use strict;
use warnings;

my %Gene_length = ('MDR', 2400,'BRAC', 2267,'Rubisco', 1700) ;
print "Key-value pairs in associative array: ", %Gene_length,"\n";
%Gene_length without quotes

Output:
Key-value pairs in associative array: BRAC2267MDR2400Rubisco1700

Chapter 6

Program E6.1

```
use strict;
use warnings;

my $a = 8;
my $b = 4;

if ($a == $b)
{
print "The value stored in \$a is less than \$b\n";
} # missing }
else
{
print "The value stored in \$a is greater than \$b\n";
}
```

Output:

The value stored in $a is greater than $b

Program E6.2

```
use strict;
use warnings;

my $a = 3;
my $b = 4;

if ($a < $b)
{
print "The value stored in \$a is less than \$b\n";
}

elsif ($a > $b)   #elseif
{
print "The value stored in \$a is greater than \$b\n";
}

else
```

```
{
print "The value stored in \$a is equal to \$b\n";
}
```

Output:
The value stored in $a is less than $b

Chapter 7

Program E7.1

```
use strict;
use warnings;

for (my $i = 0; $i <= 9; $i++)  #< missing
{
print "i = $i\n";
}
```

Output:
```
i = 0
i = 1
i = 2
i = 3
i = 4
i = 5
i = 6
i = 7
i = 8
i = 9
```

Program E7.2

```
use strict;
use warnings;

my $i = 1;
while($i <=10)
{
print "$i\n";
$i++;   #missing
}
```

Output:
```
1
2
3
4
```

```
5
6
7
8
9
10
```

Chapter 8

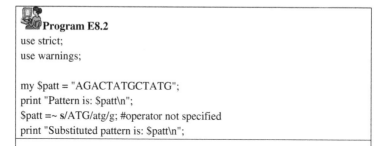

Program E8.1

```
use strict;
use warnings;

my $string = "AGCGATCGTAGTCAGTCGCATG";
if ($string =~ m/GATC/)   # ~missing
{
print "Pattern found\n";
}
else
{
print "Pattern not found\n";
}
```

Output:
Pattern found

Program E8.2

```
use strict;
use warnings;

my $patt = "AGACTATGCTATG";
print "Pattern is: $patt\n";
$patt =~ s/ATG/atg/g; #operator not specified
print "Substituted pattern is: $patt\n";
```

Output:
Pattern is: AGACTATGCTATG
Substituted pattern is: AGACTatgCTatg

Chapter 9

Program E9.1
use strict;
use warnings;

my $sequence = 'GCTGACGTACGTATGCAGTCA';
print "Sequence: $sequence\n";
my @seq_split = split/T/, $sequence; # , missing
print "After Split: @seq_split\n";

Output:
Sequence: GCTGACGTACGTATGCAGTCA
After Split: GC GACG ACG A GCAG CA

Program E9.2
use strict;
use warnings;

my $string = 'ACGTACGTATGCAGTACGTGGCTGA';
print "Sequence: $string\n";
my $sub_string = substr ($string,2,10) ; # $ missing
print "The substring retrieved is: $sub_string \n";

Output:
Sequence: ACGTACGTATGCAGTACGTGGCTGA
The substring retrieved is: GTACGTATGC

Chapter 10

Program E10.1

```
use strict;
use warnings;

my $array_ref = [4, 69, 'ATGC'];     # ] missing
print "Reference: $array_ref\n";
print "Dereference: @{$array_ref}\n";
```

Output:
Reference: ARRAY(0x967b94) #may differ in your output
Dereference: 4 69 ATGC

Program E10.2

```
use strict;
use warnings;

my $scalar = 100;
print "Scalar Value: $scalar\n";
my $scalar_ref = \$scalar;
print "Reference1: $scalar_ref\n";

my $scalar_ref1 = \$scalar_ref;
print "Reference2: $scalar_ref1\n";

print "Dereference \$scalar_ref: $$scalar_ref\n";  # $ missing
print "Dereference \$scalar_ref1: ", $$$scalar_ref1,"\n";  # $ missing
```

Output:
Scalar Value: 100
Reference1: SCALAR(0x1e834ec) #may vary in your output
Reference2: REF(0x1e835c4)   #may vary in your output
Dereference $scalar_ref: 100   #desired output
Dereference $scalar_ref1: 100   #desired output

Chapter 11

Program E11.1

```
use strict;
use warnings;

my $sum = add(4,6);
print "The sum of 4 and 6 is: $sum\n";

sub add
{
my $first = shift(@_);
my $second = shift(@_);  # value not assigned to $second
my $sum = $first + $second;
return($sum);
}
```

Output:
The sum of 4 and 6 is: 10

Program E11.2

```
use strict;
use warnings;

my @fruits = qw (Apple Banana Grapes);
my @color = qw (Red Yellow Green);
array(\@fruits, \@color);  #\ missing

sub array
{
print "Values in \@_ : @_\n";
my ($fruits, $color) = @_;
print "\@fruits values: @{$fruits}\n";
print "\@color values: @{$color}\n";
}
```

Output:
Values in @_ : ARRAY(0x5f34ec) ARRAY(0x5f34bc) #may vary

```
@fruits values: Apple Banana Grapes
@color values: Red Yellow Green
```

Chapter 12

**Program E12.1**
```
use strict;
use warnings;

my @inFile;
if(open(IN,"Triticum.fasta"))
{
@inFile = <IN>;  # use @ instead of $
print "File found\n\n";
close(IN);
}
else{
print "File not found\n";
}
print "Content of file:\n\n";
foreach my $line (@inFile)
{
print $line;
}
```

Output:
>gi|14017554|ref|NP_114241.1| ribosomal protein S16 [Triticum aestivum]
MLKLRLKRCGRKQQAVYRIVAIDVRSRREGRDLRKVGFYDPIKNQTC
LNVPAILYFLEKGAQPTRTVYDI
LRKAEFFKEKESTLS
>gi|14017555|ref|NP_114242.1| photosystem II protein K [Triticum aestivum]
MPNILSLTCICFNSVIYPTSFFFAKLPEAYAIFNPIVDFMPVIPLFFFLLAF
VWQAAVSFR
>gi|14017556|ref|NP_114243.1| photosystem II protein I [Triticum aestivum]
MLTLKLFVYTVVIFFVSLFIFGFLSNDPGRNPGREE

**Program E12.2**
```
use strict;
```

176

```
use warnings;

my $inFile = 'Triticum.fasta';
my $outFile = 'Triticum.New.fasta';
my $fileData;
open(IN,"$inFile") || die "File not found";
open(OUT,">$outFile") || die "New file not created";  # > missing

while ($fileData = <IN>)
{
print OUT "$fileData";
}
close(IN);
```

Output:
Check file in the folder

Chapter 13

Program E13.1

use strict;
use warnings;

use seq; # missing
my $DNA = 'CGATCGTAGCTAGCGACGATGC';
print "$DNA \t #DNA Sequence\n";
my $DNA_complement = complementary($DNA);
print "$DNA_complement \t #Complementary DNA Sequence\n";

Module: seq.pm
#subroutine to generate complementary DNA sequence
sub complementary
{
my $seq = shift;
$seq =~ tr/ATGC/TACG/;
return($seq);
}
1;

Output:
CGATCGTAGCTAGCGACGATGC #DNA Sequence
GCTAGCATCGATCGCTGCTACG #Complementary DNA Sequence

Program E13.2

```
use strict;
use warnings;

use modules::sequence;
my $DNA = 'CGATCGTAGCTAGCGACGATGC';
print "$DNA \t #DNA Sequence\n";
my $DNA_complement = sequence::complement($DNA);
 #module name missing from subroutine call
print "$DNA_complement \t #Complementary DNA Sequence\n";
```

Module: sequence.pm
package sequence;

```
#subroutine to generate complementary DNA sequence
sub complement
{
my $seq = shift;
$seq =~ tr/ATGC/TACG/;
return($seq);
}
1;
```

Output:
```
CGATCGTAGCTAGCGACGATGC   #DNA Sequence
GCTAGCATCGATCGCTGCTACG   #Complementary DNA Sequence
```

Suggested reading

www.perl.org

Index

www.ingramcontent.com/pod-product-compliance
Lightning Source LLC
LaVergne TN
LVHW092332060326

832902LV00008B/611